MEDITATION

Intimate Experiences with the Divine
through Contemplative Practices

Enjoy these other books in the Common Sentience series:

ANCESTORS: *Divine Remembrances of Lineage, Relations and Sacred Sites*

ANGELS: *Personal Encounters with Divine Beings of Light*

ANIMALS: *Personal Tales of Encounters with Spirit Animals*

GUIDES: *Mystical Connections to Soul Guides and Divine Teachers*

NATURE: *Divine Experiences with Trees, Plants, Stones and Landscapes*

Learn more at sacredstories.com.

MEDITATION

Intimate Experiences with the Divine
through Contemplative Practices

Featuring

SISTER DR. JENNA

SACRED STORIES
PUBLISHING

Books may be purchased through booksellers or by contacting Sacred Stories Publishing.

Editor: Gina Mazza

Meditation: Intimate Experiences with the Divine
Through Contemplative Practices
Sister Dr. Jenna

Tradepaper ISBN: 978-1-945026-91-1
EBook ISBN: 978-1-945026-92-8

Library of Congress Control Number: 2021950601

Published by Sacred Stories Publishing, Fort Lauderdale, FL USA

CONTENTS

PART THREE: DEEPENING YOUR CONNECTION TO THE DIVINE THROUGH MEDITATION

PART ONE

Understanding Meditation

The quieter you become, the more you are able to hear.

—RUMI

A TIME TO CHOOSE

———•◦●◦•———

*W*e find ourselves, right now, in the age of great transformation, one of the most consequential moments in human history. These are indeed the times that the great prophets and seers throughout the millennia have spoken about.

Mankind has experienced and survived many eras of tremendous change, of course, yet with each turn of the spiral, the permutations become more amplified—as if there will be one final revolution of the cycle that turns it all around so we can start anew once more.

Dating back 2,000 to 3,000 years ago, these hallowed seers and prophets descended on earth to illumine for us the path of love, but have we listened to them? Many centuries later, even though sacred texts have been scribed and timeless cultural and ancestral wisdom has been offered, we are still struggling just to be kind, respectful, and loving towards one another, and to be at peace with ourselves.

Why haven't we done this yet? If all the solutions have been in our midst for thousands of years, why haven't we evolved into a human culture with spiritual integrity, able to stand firm in our individual self-worth and, while in the company of others, offer them this same respect?

How many more generations must we live through while enduring violence, war, famine, poverty, rape, murder, and crisis after crisis, along with the cumulative trauma that all of this provokes? What is the missing link?

I believe that we're catapulting into this self-destructive behavior because we are so external in our approach to how we live our lives that we're not able to *hear* the answers. We're not listening to our deepest thoughts—the ones that are hidden behind our surface thoughts. The antidote for this is to take time for internal reflection without interruption, without encroachment from outside opinions, conditionings, and presuppositions.

More than ever, in this epochal time, meditation is a crucial tool. If we are not hearing ourselves and each other anymore through the din of our modern lifestyle, meditation and other contemplative practices offer the means to slow down and listen to these innermost nudges that are quietly signaling to us who and what we really are—a soul—and why we're actually here in this human world. If we can carry *that* understanding inside of our personalities, we might just be able to save ourselves and each other a lot of wasted time and energy . . . and possibly save ourselves altogether.

We are a species that knows how to reinvent ourselves, and how to progress. One need only look at history to see evidence of how ingenuity has moved us forward—the past few hundred years, for example, brought forth agricultural, industrial, and technological revolutions.

At this early turn of the 21st century, we are in the industry of self-reflection, introspection, and spiritual searching. The old ways of being and doing aren't going to get us where we are destined to go now. We must dig deep and catch those genuine jewels of thought, and meditation is the most direct route to that insight.

Right now, our human population is being given the power of choice to either continue down the path of tragedy, or to finally, ultimately learn that we are here to love, and to choose the path of spiritual development and enlightenment.

These past few years, in particular, have been challenging. If anything, it has forced us to be more reflective and, as a result, more of us are experiencing mystical moments in which we're seeing ourselves in a different way and our existence in a different light. Many of us have lost loved ones, our livelihoods, and daily routines that we've always relied on for security and comfort.

We have no idea what the future holds. Some of us know *what* to do but just don't have the internal strength to do it. Yet with a consistent practice of reflection and listening to the thoughts inside, while being sensitive to our feelings and emotions, we can prepare for whatever is coming next and get ourselves safely to our eventual destination.

Where can meditation and contemplation take us? Imagine if more of us—a majority, perhaps—led with patience, cooperation, and forgiveness. What would our lives be like? The personal stories on these pages offer a taste of this, but first, let's turn inward to explore this mystical experience of meditation.

THE EXPERIENCE OF
GOD INSIDE YOU

———••●●●••———

On some level, everybody meditates. To say that you have never meditated or don't know how to do it simply isn't true. Every one of us is naturally wired to have private, quiet, mindful moments in which we spontaneously review our lives to see if there is something better we can reach for.

Similarly, we've all had mystical moments that enable us to transcend the ego, greed, lust, the need for security, and other limitations, and experience the Divinity within.

So, the first question I ask anyone who is beginning a contemplative practice is, "Do you know that you *already* meditate?" Can you remember a moment when you were going through a hard time and turned inward to find the solution? Chances are, you have, and this ability to self-reflect becomes more of a practice once you awaken to it and want to sustain it.

As I've gone deeper into what meditation has meant for my own life, it's definitely a coming home to the real essence of who I am. I can only be who I am if I'm honest with myself. That is all that any of us can do. Meditation opens that window of self-honesty, which is the virtue we all need in order to navigate through the interweaving of experiences that are carried inside the soul.

WHAT IS MEDITATION?

Meditation, therefore, is this intimate journey of coming home to the essential part of you that is beyond your titles, labels, and roles, and what society and your environment distracts you from. It gives you a chance to listen to those deeper, innermost thoughts that are directly connected to the purity and presence of the Divine.

Just imagine how your existence would change if your thoughts were connected not to the mundane aspects of life, but to the sacredness of Source. Everything elevates to a higher level: the sparkle of your personality, the words you speak, the way your eyes reflect peace, the choices you make, even the way you dress, the way you take care of yourself, how you are present in your relationships. It all refines and uplifts.

Putting meditation into practice is when this private, intimate relationship with the Divine becomes the catalyst to bring forth, through your singular personality, what the world is inherently yearning for—one of simplicity, laughter, abundance, and vibrancy. These traits emerge because the soul receives energy from its intimate connection with Source.

The highest role of meditation is not only a return to love, but more specifically, a return to a sacred quality of Love. Sometimes we take for granted the power of these four letters. With a place in your life for contemplation, you begin to ponder, *Well, I know what human love feels like, but what about sacred Love, which has an energy that is far greater?* When two human beings become intimate, they tend to feel alive in their moments together, but later on, it dies down. When your heart and soul merge with Source, there is no dying down; there's only a climbing up and an expansion of the energy of sublimeness that begins to surround you.

So, meditation is really about building and forming a deeper experience of sacred Love, which melts away all that is impure. What is not sacred is hidden in the dark. Meditation illuminates Love through you, and when anyone comes into your presence, they feel this sacredness and feel safe.

This is what our world needs now, the kind of Love that has the capacity to send good wishes, share pure feelings, think kind thoughts, and do things without asking for anything in return. It's the kind of Love that can see in advance what your needs are and fulfill them before you even ask. Cultivating this expression of Love is perhaps the greatest benefit of meditation, both personally and collectively.

Before we go any further, I'd like to clear up a few misconceptions. First, it's important for us to now understand the interpretation of God in a more refined way. You will notice that I use the words God, the Divine, Source, and other terms interchangeably. I am not referring to a religious God, as in one that belongs to Hinduism, Christianity, Judaism, Islam, or others. We cannot squeeze God into a religion. He is much too big for that.

I have dear friends who are high up in the Islamic tradition, the Christian tradition, the Judaic tradition, and we regularly come together and talk. I find that many are attached to the language that's connected to their particular tradition. The most important question is, "How do we bypass all of that?" Yes, you have your deep wisdom traditions and religious beliefs, but *are you feeling God*? What's your practical, daily experience? What do you carry with you as a result of them?

Each of us has the freedom to consider God in a personal and unique way, or refute the existence of a supreme being altogether. Those who do may still have supernatural and coincidental experiences in their lives. Even atheists can meditate because I believe they take issue more with the concept of an organized structure that claims to *know* God and have power *over*

God. This leads to confusion and disappointment because if God exists, we wonder, shouldn't everything be grand? There shouldn't be war, genocide, hatred, or the suffering of millions of people around the world, but there is.

Understanding the energy of God as an unlimited consciousness of love, peace, purity, and wisdom doesn't require a religious context, or even a belief system. It requires only an open mind and the bravery to allow your mind to sift through concepts that may seem ineffable. This deeper and more accepting experience of the Divine would eradicate much of the infighting amongst even people of faith.

If your connection to your Creator is a personal and intimate one, then it doesn't belong to any religion. Maybe an organization, church, synagogue, or mosque doesn't own your contemplative moments for you. For this same reason, I think it's important to break the myth that you need to join a meditation group or study with a particular lineage in order to meditate.

There is value in doing so, if this is your desire or calling, and having a structure can help to discipline the mind, but it's not required to define yourself as someone who meditates. Now let's dive deeper into the purpose of integrating this into your life, and what results when you live from this more refined place.

HOW TO MEDITATE . . . AND WHY

editation will save your life. How so? It gives you the discernment to recognize the thoughts that are true from those that are an illusion. When you can't tell a diamond from a cubic zirconia, so to speak, you can get tricked, be fooled, self-sabotage, and end up with a great sense of loss.

Developing the ability to listen to your thoughts to see where they belong is crucial. If they belong to the true essence of the Self, which is a Love that is sacred in you, and if these thoughts are based on the purity of the soul, the direction of your life takes on an entirely different shimmer. I ask you to again imagine what your life could be like if you were willing to allow these pure thoughts to come into your decision making, into the way you maneuver in your relationships, into how you earn and spend your money, or just in the way you interpret life around you. Sit with this for a moment before reading ahead to the next paragraph.

When your experiences of meditation and contemplation are rooted in this kind of intentional observation and awareness, it's saving your life because it mitigates the struggle. You give up the addiction that life has to be hard and filled with obstacles. Whenever difficulties arise, you stop pointing the finger at another for the reason why you're miserable. Meditation helps you to realize that you—and only you—are the creator of your life narrative. It wakes you up to self-responsibility as a birthright, not a burden.

Moments of meditation can be captured either in stillness or when you're in action, whether taking care of your family, making a cup of tea, leading your team at work, or even walking from one room to the next. These moments often arise for me when I see someone's face in the midst of a conversation, because I'm looking at what's at the base of my intent for speaking my words as it relates to this person in front of me—is there judgment or is there a blessing?

When you consider what's going on in the world right now, having just this goal to be much more thoughtful when encountering another would have a powerful effect. I don't mean to say that all would be perfect. There still needs to be an element of *I don't know me* because that element gives you the opportunity to be curious about life, and the humility to learn from others. So, the goal of meditation is not perfection, but rather, clarity of mind, and purity of heart.

STAGES OF MEDITATION

One of the myths about meditation is that you have to do it for 30 minutes in the morning or evening, light a candle or incense, hold a rosary or mala, recite a mantra, or read scripture. These are aspects of meditation that can make it more reverent for you, but even after doing these practices, it's important to observe, *Where are my thoughts?* When you're reaching for your smartphone, opening the fridge, getting the children ready for school, putting one leg into your pants and then the other, where are your thoughts? Are you in the present moment, or are you in your past or the future?

My approach to meditation derives from Raja Yoga, the practice of the Brahma Kumaris. It is a process that is simple, easy to follow, and that anyone can do. When I speak about how to meditate, I begin with discussing these stages because they are universal and true to every human being.

The first steps in preparation for meditation are *relaxation* and *concentration*. In these practices, you begin to observe then let go of the tension and stress of everyday life, and redirect the mind and body to a state of calm by focusing on your breath and that core question, *Where are my thoughts?*

The next stage is *contemplation,* or reflecting deeply on yourself, your inner world, your values, and what is going on in your life currently. If there's a relationship that's challenging you, for example, place what you are going through in front of the Divine in the form of contemplation.

After a while of doing this, you will eventually reach the next stage, which is a place of *stillness.* This is where the soul settles, and is in a mode of receptivity for what it needs to help you claim your power, deal with a situation in front of you, or to continue amplifying whatever you are becoming.

The role of contemplation is to till the soil and climb to a higher dimension. Stillness is where you're open and giving permission to Source to fill you with everything that needs to be filled. When you come back into your five senses after a period of contemplation and stillness, the soul is now in motion. It carries the current of the fresh experience that has been captured from the Divine in those moments.

The next stage is *realization,* or when your self-understanding and feelings combine, and you begin to experience a profound, more meaningful reality within. The final stage is actual *meditation,* in which you are remembering your eternal identity and reawakening a profound sense of wellbeing.

Regardless of the stage, the core aspect of this process is when your conscious thoughts slow down and are linked to the understanding of God being this supreme ocean of love and peace, and you realize that the energy of the Divine will never judge you or hold anything against you. It just wants to keep giving power to your soul so that it can reclaim its original essence, value, and worth.

As you experience meditation on increasingly deeper levels, you will eventually enter the *incorporeal* stage, where you're not conscious anymore of the thoughts connected to your five senses. You're just the soul, that sentient being of light. That energy of the soul is so vibrant, so powerful. When you're conscious of your energy as a soul in your body, and begin to have access to it, you become able to continue pulling in that orb of unconditional love and light from the Divine. You surrender and are open to receiving sacred Love. The vibrations from God just keep flowing through you and eventually when you do this process once, twice, five times, a hundred times, a thousand times, it develops a natural, innate sense of truth and Divinity.

Relating this back to the condition of our world, I sense and see that we're not pulling the energy of God's love into us enough. We are, but not enough. And remember, my interpretation of God isn't a religious one but an energy of love, peace, wisdom, truth, and power.

Now, if all of you, dear readers, can pause again, right here, and just think on that for as long as you can, now and in your days going forward, I guarantee that eventually you'll experience a shift in your consciousness. This shift brings forth the humility to say, "I need this remembrance and experience of sacred Love, because if I don't have it as my internal compass, how am I going to survive in the outside world?"

LIVING THE EXPERIENCE OF MEDITATION

I don't think that many people in my current life know that in my twenties, I owned two popular nightclubs on Miami Beach. I share more about this time in my life in Part Two, so for now I will just say that back then, I used to go to bed around the same time that I now awake in the morning to meditate.

We'd close down the clubs around five o'clock in the morning and maybe go for breakfast, then I'd head home to crash in bed, and get up around noon. Every day, I'd repeat the cycle: Take a shower, get myself ready, have brunch with friends, and hang at the clubs for the rest of the day and night. It was an existence that focused on my dress, my physical appearance, where I lived, the fancy cars I drove, the men I dated, and who was with me in my social life. All of that was coming from a particular consciousness that the world gives permission for and says is okay. I thought that that's what life was all about . . . and I still don't see anything wrong with it, as I believe it's only unhealthy when you compromise your sense of self-worth and values to live a particular lifestyle.

Today, I find myself in the teachings of Raja Yoga, and I'm asked to rise at four o'clock in the morning to meditate. I remembered my parents doing all of this during my teenage years, and was very inspired by them, but in early adult years, I hadn't considered that meditation was going to be my life. Yet something was recorded on my soul about the sacredness of those uninterrupted early morning hours. In later years, I would come to love listening to the soft whisper of God's wisdom in the air every morning at dawn, and I still do.

Of course, living the experience of meditation is not confined to a practice or bound by time. It is always a part of you and your thoughts. I have conditioned myself to pause every hour, on the hour, to just check if I am *Om Shanti*, which means *I am peace*, and if I am connected—meaning, is the energy of the Divine moving me, or are my desires moving me? The Brahma Kumaris call this process traffic control, because it enables you to stop the traffic in your mind and check where you are. You might need to get off this exit or keep going down the path you're on. These traffic-light moments keep us on course and give us the ability to redirect, if needed.

This hourly check-in takes care of even my little, limited human desires, but if I'm being moved by my desires with an absence of that fragrance of the intent of God's vibration, then I'm going to eventually run into challenges, struggles, and obstacles. Even on days when I am extremely busy, which there are many, in the midst of it all, I pause every hour for a minute or two or three, and reconnect to my truth.

Meditation can permeate life in this way. The moment you open your eyes, give thanks before you eat a meal, before you fall asleep at night, anytime you have a moment of anxiety or indecision and want to know the best way forward; and certainly, when you are feeling frustrated, lonely, exhausted, or hopeless, turn to the One who is always there for you. These are all ripe meditative moments.

I want to re-emphasize that this is not necessarily easy and seamless. Our souls carry an accumulation of experiences that affect our thoughts and choices. What I can tell you is that there's nothing sweeter than being kind, thoughtful, open, and generous. Even if you are a spitfire, or you've lost your cool, or feel like a mess and are toppled upside down, be very open and honest about it in your meditative moments. Give it to God, and you will become right side up.

In the secular and even the spirituality worlds, a lot of people seem to believe that a successful meditation is one in which you have no thoughts. I don't personally agree with that. I've seen a lot of people shy away from meditation when they hear that they have to empty the mind, as it feels like an impossible task. And it is, I believe, because the soul is an immortal, eternal, imperishable energy of light that is carrying many, many, many lifetimes of experiences inside of it. How can you turn off all of these experiences? How do you do that when there's so much in you that wants to express?

To me, a successful meditation is where you've applied the right thoughts with the right interpretation of the experience in front of you, and it makes you into a stronger person. It's more like this: You listen, you respond, you listen again, and you receive. You listen, you respond, you listen again, and you receive. That receiving is where your answers are coming from, and those answers are all thoughts. That is why you can't empty your mind in meditation . . . or shouldn't!

Life happens, right? Because the soul is in the body of the five senses, you want concrete answers to life's challenges. You need to know how to relate to your spouse who is vibrating at a completely different level now after 10 years of marriage. You need to deal with your son or daughter who is going through puberty and is no longer the sweet, innocent child you knew as a toddler. You have to deal with a relative who's jealous of you and needs to get over it. The bills need to be paid, and the house needs to be maintained. On top of all of that, you must respond to a society, a government, a country, and the way the world is functioning, and your place in it. And you can't handle any of that if your mind is empty and you're not thinking. It requires a relationship between the soul and Source.

When someone says to me, "Sister Jenna, I don't know how you do all that you do," my response is simple: On my own, I cannot do it, but if I pull the light of Divine Love into myself, I can do anything.

So, I ask those who are not meditating, "From where are you pulling your energy?" From a partner, from society, from social media, from how you look in the mirror? All of these things are physical and outside of you. The opposite would be pulling your energy from the Divine qualities of love, peace, purity, truth, and joy. You're in your marriage; how do you respond in love? You're dealing with your teenager; how do you respond with joy? You're talking to a jealous sibling; how do you respond in truth? You're actively engaged in social causes; how do you respond in peace? Do you see now how meditation becomes a tool that can save you?

So, the purpose of meditation is to give you insights into yourself, into Source, into our true humanity, and into everyday life. It can be subtly in the background of your private daily thoughts, or in the foreground as an evolved practice. Either way, there is an exquisite art in being able to see and feel the energy of God in another child of God, and in every living being. Drawing from my disco years, I understand now the delicate and sweet dance between our visible and invisible worlds, if only we're open to learning this inner choreography.

WHAT HAPPENS WHEN YOU MEDITATE?

———••●●●••———

suspect that a lot of people are having mystical experiences but don't realize it, or don't have the language for it—although many in this book have captured it beautifully. These unforgettable moments are indisputable and are recorded on the soul forever.

I wonder how many walk in the world with these experiences so privately. It's certainly not something that is talked about in many everyday settings, like in a business meeting. We don't sit around the boardroom, ready to cut a half-million-dollar deal, and share with our colleagues, "Oh, did I tell you what happened to me when I was six years old and saw the light of the Divine through my inner vision?" Perhaps we should.

I've had the blessing of being around many female yogi powerhouses who are spiritual representatives within the Brahma Kumaris. I've watched them closely over many years and what I've looked for as a personal teaching is the way they show up. What I've observed is that they consistently carry within them a balance of love and law, of the spiritual and the physical, of silence and speaking wisdom. Everything they do comes down to, *How can I help?* They are not attached to the ego consciousness of I-me-mine; this kind of thinking is very reduced in their personalities. These women have made an impact on me such that I want to become this. I want to be pure and clean in my intentions, as they are.

Now that I've been on my spiritual journey for about 30 years as a progeny of that culture, and modeling what I've observed, I can say that I would not choose to do anything else but live a life of generosity for others and for concerns beyond myself. The ego is still there, and God knows I need to reduce more of that vibration in my personality, but I'm not going to negate that the Divine has poured a great amount of love, sincerity, and humility into me through my spiritual teacher, Baba, and will continue to pour into me.

I share all of these thoughts because this is what happens when you consistently meditate. You are inspired to become increasingly kind, generous, loving, and less dictated by the ego. It happens subtly over time, like a rose blooming inside you, eventually sharing its fragrance with anyone who comes into contact with you.

Those who give devotion to contemplative practices develop an inner power about them, a gracious spirit, a strength that cannot be hidden yet is not offensive or intimidating. It transforms the personality that you're traveling with in this world, and is a great neutralizer. You become more resilient, centered, solid, and at peace with yourself. This is priceless, because when challenges come up, which they will, you're not shaken just because things are not going your way. Instead, you pause and ask yourself, *What is this trying to teach me? What am I being asked to look at?* Your responses become more tolerant, adaptive, and alert. Regardless of what happens in the day-to-day, the sweetness of love and power of bliss remain alive inside.

You may not have yogis or elders or spiritual mentors in your life, but you do have *you*. What I mean is that contemplative practices deepen that part of you that is able to be in quietude, whether cutting vegetables, going for a walk, or driving in your car. Turning within enables you to feel the real part of your personality, the sacred and most essential part, when it comes knocking on the door of your mind wanting your attention.

I am thinking now of my dear mother, who has been a major influence on me, and continues to be. Even though my mother is older and has dementia, her energy of divinity is not hidden in all of the insane things that she does on any given day due to her health condition. Quite the opposite: The fragrance of her attainment remains clearly visible, as she has pulled so much of God's love into herself over the course of her life. So, it doesn't matter if she's eating the leaf off a plant on the coffee table, or looking at family photos and wanting to feed the people in the pictures because she thinks they are hungry; through it all, the energy of the Divine is what shines through, and she continues to inspire everyone around her. That sense of grace, once acquired through a contemplative life, never leaves you, no matter what.

Much of the meditative experience *is* mystical, and it almost feels like an injustice to ask the ego to decode what the Divine is doing through your consciousness, because it's far deeper than words can express. That is why I am in awe of the contributing authors on the following pages who have managed to convey their intimate experiences with Source in their own words.

So, settle in, take a deep breath before turning the page . . . and savor these indelible meditation moments from individuals just like you.

PART TWO

Intimate Experiences with the Divine
through Contemplative Practices

Contemplation is life itself, fully awake, fully active, and fully aware that it is alive. It is spiritual wonder.

—THOMAS MERTON

DIVINITY AT THE LAUNDROMAT

*I*t was an otherwise ordinary afternoon. Having accompanied my mother to the laundromat in New York City, I was partly occupied in my own little contemplative inner world, as most six-year-olds typically are.

Surrounded by the hum of washing machines slushing loads of clothes, and rows of dryers tossing them about behind tiny, round-glass windows, I was innocently playing with a doll or other toy, while my mother folded laundry on a metal table.

Spontaneously, my consciousness was transported to somewhere far, far away from the store I was in, playing next to my mom.

Quite vividly, I saw my little girl self, in this alternative realm, surrounded by a council of highly elevated men and women. Dressed all in white, they looked more like pure beings of light. As I ascended upward and as they held me in this pure Divine light, I had a sense that these benevolent and powerful beings were bringing me to this higher state of awareness because they wanted to check on me, like they were my true guardians.

The feeling came over me that this council of protectors loved me dearly. It's as if they were just touching in to see where I was on the physical plane, and making sure I was doing okay. This vision completely awed me, yet I had no context for it or even a care about what was occurring, or why. I experienced it as a connection to Divine Love, pure and simple.

After some moments—I don't know how many—my consciousness returned to my physical body enough that I was able to tug on my mother's skirt to get her attention.

"What is it, honey?" she asked, placing a pile of folded sheets into a laundry basket.

"I don't feel like I'm here," I said.

"What do you mean?" she responded.

"I don't know. I feel weird."

"It's okay, dear. It's alright. Come."

And with that, she took my hand, hoisted the basket under her arm, and led me out of the laundromat to make our way back home.

As we walked the city streets, I realized that my mother was totally oblivious to what had just happened to me, and I didn't have the language to either discern or define what it was. So, I said nothing. My tendency while growing up was to not do anything to add to my mother's stress, so I never did ask her about this event in the years to follow.

In those days, life was not easy for my mom. Given the trauma that had occurred in her life—she was orphaned at the age of seven and suffered through a lot of abuse and violence—my mother walked through her days feeling mostly scared, somewhat aimless, and routinely unaware of what the next day would offer her. She was just trying to survive as a single mom, and to make a life for us.

About four years after the laundromat experience, I witnessed my mother having a full-on nervous breakdown. My only recollection is of her lying down, screaming relentlessly, then being rushed into a car. After that, I didn't see mom for a long while. Somewhere in the recesses of my being, I had a sense that enduring this startling episode was a necessary precursor to my life's work of bringing souls to God so they could be healed.

After my spiritual journey began in my twenties, and as I was led to the Brahma Kumaris, that mystical encounter from age six began to resurface in my awareness. I somehow found myself making reference to it again and again. As I learned about the founder, Brahma Baba, and the other elders who have passed into Spirit, the experience clicked into place in my mind and heart.

Finally, I understood that this council of spiritual teachers was indeed checking on me as a child, knowing that I would one day be a part of this spiritual community, and would help to lead it worldwide. In fact, I believe it is why I felt an immediate resonance and deep soul link with the Brahma Kumaris, and why meeting them felt like coming home to both my ancestral and spiritual family.

I carry those moments in the laundromat with me to this day, and believe that every one of us in this earthly world has a council in Spirit looking out for us, if only we are willing to receive them in our hearts.

Sister Dr. Jenna

CHICKIE AND THE PATH
OF AWAKENING

We were both pups when my parents got her—I, about 18 months old; she, somewhat younger, but older by far in wisdom and experience. She had already had a brief career in the movies, having played one of Daisy's puppies in the *Dagwood and Blondie* series; but now, too old for the part, she had been given to my comedy-writer father in lieu of payment for a script he had turned in.

Her name was Chickie, and she was a wonderful mix of Welsh corgi and bearded collie. A white star blazed on her chest, and she had four white feet and a white-tipped tail to complement her long, black fur. Even though she was scarcely over a year old, she was already motherly and sat by my crib for hours on end, making sure that no harm would come to me. If I cried, she would be off to my mother, insisting that she come immediately. If I wanted to play, she would bring toys—hers, as well as mine. Chickie seemed to be virtue incarnate, a Saint Francis of Assisi of dogs, who took on responsibilities of a saintly cast. I thought of her as my sister and, with all our travels, my constant and closest friend.

Chickie and I took to having long jaunts with each other. We would be gone for hours at a time, and either my parents were too busy to notice or they trusted Chickie's care of me. With Chickie in charge, I was given a great deal of freedom to wander in a world as miraculous as it was marvelous.

Behind our house was a large wooded area where Chickie and I began what I have come to think of as our travels in awakening. Two hours with Chickie in the woods yielded an incredible range of learnings. Chickie was more nose than eyes, and I quite the other way around; but together we investigated the endless treasures of forest and meadow. I remember crawling on four legs to follow more closely her interests and discoveries. As she sniffed out deer scat, mice holes, squirrel trails, and bug routes, she would occasionally turn around and check with me to see if I saw them too.

Chickie taught me to be alert to both the seen and the unseen, the heard and the unheard. A whisper of wings would turn her head, and mine would follow, waiting for the flutter that would finally announce to my human-hindered head, *Bird on the wing!* Chickie would lift her nose, her tail would signal attention, and we would be off and running to follow the adventures of the air—entrancing molecules luring us to destinies both savory and dangerous.

Chickie gave me metaphors for my later life's work, especially when it came to digging. Paws scratching away at apparently nothing soon revealed dark secrets hidden in the earth—old bones, ancient feathers, and things so mysterious as to be beyond human knowing. Years later, I would probe and dig into the soil of the human subconscious with something like Chickie's fervor to find there the bones of old myths, the feathers of essence, and the great mysterious matrix that still sustains and lures the human quest.

For years, Chickie served as the center for calm and a kind of spiritual tranquility in our life of constant change brought about through my Dad's work, as well as his penchant for eccentric adventures. Even though I went to something like 20 different schools all over the country before I was 12, I would always come home to Chickie, who regarded all of life as delightful and who maintained a saintly comportment and stability in the face of any whimsy we humans could invent.

Chickie also taught me my best lessons in ethics and responsibility. She seemed to have little self-interest. Many of her actions were clearly for others. She was empathy personified, whether in consoling me when I was upset or in the way she would listen to humans as they railed against their supposed fate. Her answer was simply to be there, to place her head upon their knee and look at them sweetly in the eye, her gaze unblinking and never wavering.

Chickie accompanied me on the most important experience of my entire lifetime—that of the spiritual epiphany . . . my key experience in awakening. It happened in my sixth year. I had been sent to Catholic school in Brooklyn. My father had been tossed off *The Bob Hope Show* for an excess of high spirits. We were broke and living with my mother's Sicilian parents in the Italian section of that noble, if bad-mouthed, borough.

Theologically precocious and buttressed with questions designed by my agnostic father, I would assail the little nun who taught our first grade with queries that seemed logical to me but blasphemous to her.

"Sister Theresa, when Ezekiel saw the wheel, was he drunk?" Or, "Sister Theresa, how do you know that Jesus wasn't walking on rocks below the surface when he seemed to be walking on the water?" And, "Sister Theresa, when Jesus rose, was that because God filled him full of helium?"

Then there was the day of the question that tipped her dogma, as well as her dignity. It had to do with Jesus' natural functions and whether he ever had to go to the toilet. Her response was to jump on a stool and tack up a large sheet of heavy cardboard, and in large India-ink letters wrote JEAN HOUSTON'S YEARS IN PURGATORY.

All further theological questions of an original bent met with the little nun X-ing in more years for me to endure in purgatory. By the last day of the first grade, I had accumulated something like 300 million years in purgatory to my credit.

Spiritually bereft, I told my father about the debacle and he, finding it very funny, took me off immediately to see the motion picture *The Song of Bernadette*. This famous movie is renowned for its scenes of Saint Bernadette's vision of the holy Madonna in the grotto at Lourdes, which thereafter became a famous place for healing. Unfortunately, during the holiest of scenes, with the Virgin Mary appearing in luminous white in the grotto before the praying Bernadette, my father burst into laughter, as he had known the starlet cast in the role of Mary and found some humor in her playing it. Leaving the theatre in a state of embarrassment with my father still laughing, I wanted to quickly get home in order to emulate Bernadette's remarkable vision.

My destination was a guest room with a very deep closet that looked a lot like a grotto. There were no clothes in the closet, for Chickie had commandeered it as a nest for her new eight puppies. I explained my need to Chickie, feeling that she would not mind my moving her pups, being as she would want me to open a space for the greatest Mama of them all to show up. When she protested mildly, I further explained that I didn't want the Holy Mother to step on her pups. After that, Chickie watched my actions with interest.

Kneeling in the now cleared Brooklyn "grotto", I prayed to the Madonna to show up in the closet as she had for Bernadette at Lourdes. I began by closing my eyes and counting slowly to 10, while promising to give up candy for two weeks if she would only show up. I opened my eyes to encounter the Madonna Chickie lovingly carrying one of her pups back into the grotto. I kept on counting to ever higher numbers, promising all manner of food sacrifices—mostly my favorite Sicilian delicacies like chicken with lemon and garlic sauce—but my revelation was only to see more and more puppies back in the closet.

Finally, I counted to a very high number, 167, and having given up all calories, I told the Holy Mother that I could not think of anything else to give up, so would she please, please, please show up as I really wanted to see her.

This time I was sure that she would make it. I opened my eyes, and there was Chickie contentedly licking all eight of her puppies.

"Oh, Chickie," I sighed and reached out to pat her, whereupon she bestowed on me a kindly lick and a compassionate look as if I were her ninth puppy.

At that moment came a vague spiritual forewarning, as if I had prayed for the Madonna and seen her in one of her many forms in Chickie, the all wise, all loving mother and her care for her pups. But still I yearned for the movie version and did not yet recognize the truth of what I had been given . . . and she Herself offered me another chance. In a dreamy, unspecified state, I went over to the window seat and looked at the fig tree blooming in our yard . . . and suddenly it all happened—the most important awakening state of my entire life.

In my innocence, I must have unwittingly tapped into the appropriate spiritual doorway, for suddenly the key turned and the door to the universe opened. Nothing changed in my outward perceptions. There were no visions, no sprays of golden light, certainly no appearance by the standard brand Madonna. The world remained as it had been. Yet everything around me, including myself, moved into meaning.

My mind awakened to a consciousness that spanned centuries and was on intimate terms with the universe—everything now mattered. Just as Chickie had taught me, everything was interesting and important: deer scat, old leaves, spilled milk, my Mary Jane shoes, the fig tree, the smell of glue on the back of the gold paper stars I had just pasted on the wall paper, the stars themselves, my grandfather Prospero Todaro's huge stomach, the chipped paint on the ceiling, my Nana's special stuffed artichokes, my father's typewriter, the silky ears of corn in a Texas cornfield, my *Dick and Jane* reader, and all the music that ever was—all were in a state of resonance and of the most immense and ecstatic kinship.

I was in a universe of friendship and fellow feeling, a companionable universe filled with interwoven Presence and the dance of life. This went on forever, but it was only about two seconds, for the plane that I saw out the window had moved only slightly across the sky. I had entered into timelessness, the domain in which eternity was the only reality and a few seconds could seem like forever.

Only in reflection have I come to realize how much of what I then felt and knew had been prepared for me by Chickie and her guidance in the ways of awakening. All those rambles that we took together were now one ramble, all the smells and sights of nature to which she had introduced me were present along with the fig tree blooming in the yard, Chickie herself and her pups in the closet, the plane in the sky, the sky itself, and even my idea of the Madonna. All had become part of a single unity, a glorious symphonic resonance in which every part of the universe was an illuminated part of everything else, and I knew that in some way it all worked together, and it was very good.

Somewhere downstairs, I heard the door slam, and my father entered the house laughing. Instantly, the whole universe joined in. Great roars of hilarity sounded from sun to sun. Field mice tittered, and so did angels and rainbows. Even Chickie seemed to be chuckling. Laughter leavened every atom and every star until I saw a universe inspirited and spiraled by joy, not unlike the one I read of years later in the *Divine Comedy*, when Dante described his great vision in paradise: *D'el Riso d'el Universo*, or the joy that spins the universe. This was a knowledge of the way everything worked. It worked through love and joy and the utter interpenetration and union of everything with the All That Is.

"Madonna, Madonna! Show up, show up!" I had shouted.

And the Madonna . . . Chickie . . . was at the center of it all.

Jean Houston

PRANA GIRL

"Just close your eyes and listen to my voice," the man in front of the large auditorium instructed.

"We're going to take a slow, deep breath to a count of five. Feel your belly rise as you inhale. One, two, three, four, five. Now, let it go at the same rate."

The instructor began to count again as I shifted my weight on the mat to get more comfortable. *This isn't so bad*, I thought, as I followed along. The instructor continued to speak in a soft, pleasing tone, leading us through various types of breathing techniques.

"Now exhale in short rapid bursts."

As he demonstrated this breathwork, the sound of his exhalations startled me. I opened my eyes just as he was beginning round two. This time, his breathing mixed with the chorus of the room. *This is crazy!* I thought. *They all must know what the heck they're doing.* I giggled as I watched everyone's abdomens move in and out.

This is so weird. What am I even doing here? I closed my eyes again. *Well, it's only an hour. Hang in there.*

More breaths. *I guess it's not so bad.*

More rapid breathing patterns. *Crap! I feel lightheaded. Please don't pass out, Teresa.*

"Okay, now I want you to reach behind and feel for your mat. Once you find it, go ahead and lie down."

Thank God!

"Now breathe like this . . . in, in, in . . . then push it out in one long breath."

The more I focused and followed along, the less bothered I was by the hissing of everyone's forced breaths. Continuing with the practice a bit longer, the instructor's voice subtly faded into the background.

At some point, I no longer felt like I was in an auditorium surrounded by countless strangers. My body began to rock and sway, as if the floor beneath my mat had transformed into water, sending me afloat on soothing ocean waves. Peace came over me as I drifted deeper and deeper.

Then something in the corner of the room caught my eye. A girl. *What's she doing here?* I felt drawn to this small child who couldn't have been more than five or six years old. Sitting alone in the dark corner, her long, unbrushed brown hair draped down the back of her white nightgown. Her forehead rested on her knees, and a slight shuddering of her shoulders made me sense that she was crying.

I couldn't see her face but instantly knew who she was—or, at least, I knew her emotions all too well. Watching her cower and hide, my instinct was to coddle her in my arms and hold her close. As I did so, we became one. Me, her. Her, me. Her pain filled and consumed me with a distant familiarity. Scared . . . sad . . . alone and unloved.

Unloved. She's unloved. That's what she's feeling. That poor little girl.

My tears began to flow as I held her tighter.

"I'm here for you, Teresa. I'm here," I whispered through sniffles. "I know you feel alone, but I'm here now. You're not alone."

Yet she *was* alone, and I knew it. I *hadn't* been there for her when she needed me. An overwhelming sadness filled me, causing more tears to come on full force. My body shook and shivered as I began to bawl. Loud cries bellowed from deep within me, filling the room. I couldn't stop them, nor did I want to. Tears from the little girl. Tears from me now as an adult. Tears that had been trapped inside for years. *Why doesn't Mama love me? Why is she so mean to me?*

Aw, I love that little girl. I love her. I squeezed a little tighter. *Wait a minute. She's me! I love me!* More loud cries. *I'm so sad for her. I wish I could've been there for you. I'm here. I'm here for you now.*

Then I could no longer see her face or feel her in my arms. Suddenly, the little girl was gone. She'd disappeared as fast as she came, but I still felt her emotions. I felt everything . . . every bit of pain that had been locked inside for all those years was now breaking the surface of those waves.

I'm here, I repeated. *I wish I could have always been here for you.*

A warm, soothing sensation washed over my body and a brightness passed through my closed eyelids, like a ray of light swirling over me, bathing me. *God? Is that you?*

The ringing of a bell entered my consciousness . . . then another ring, signaling the end of our meditation. Taking one last long breath, I slowly opened my eyes.

Dr. Teresa Van Woy

GRAND COSMIC LIGHT SHOW

knew something was wrong even before I read the email from my friend. Like a high-tech version of the proverbial phone call in the middle of the night, she shared that her brother had been ill with abdominal pain and was losing weight for no reason.

"His color is bad," she wrote.

This alarmed me because being jaundice—along with his other symptoms—fits the textbook description of pancreatic cancer. As a family physician, I seldom encounter patients with pancreatic cancer, but I know it can be an oppositional-defiant malignancy. It tends to resist conventional treatment like surgery, chemotherapy, and radiation, and it likes to move around. You never know when or where it might pop up next.

Sure enough, in the case of my friend's brother, scans suggested that the cancer had spread to his liver, and a biopsy confirmed it.

"Please pray for my brother's healing, and for his wife and children," she wrote. "Pray for comfort and strength, for mercy and grace."

I was willing to honor my friend's request, but there was one problem: Prayer doesn't seem to work very well for me. While most people I know believe in its power, I've learned to not expect an answer. My skepticism started years ago when my father went into the hospital for surgery to repair a blocked artery in his leg. I thought he'd be home in a couple of days. I hadn't considered that he might die there, but post-operative complications landed him in the Intensive Care Unit, surrounded by pumps and monitors.

As I sat by his hospital bed, seeing him with a tube down his throat, and intravenous lines running into his arms and neck, I begged God to heal him. I prayed that his blood pressure would stabilize, his lungs would mend, his eyes would open, and he would be fine.

I prayed against all odds for his recovery because I'd been taught that God had the power to do things like restore sight to a blind man. If He willed it, He could answer my prayer . . . but He didn't. He let my father suffer, and He made me watch. At least, that's how I saw it. I watched as my father's heart failed, his lungs filled with fluid, and his kidneys shut down.

When I said my final good-bye to my father, I bid farewell to prayer, too.

In the coming years, I went searching for other answers. I explored Buddhism with its emphasis on inner transformation, compassion for all beings, and freedom from attachment to worldly things. I learned about Taoism's teachings of the unity and mystery of the universe, the sanctity of life, and living in harmony with nature. I connected with energy healers and learned to chant, visualize auras, and breathe. I explored quantum theory and what it tells us about the nature and power of consciousness. I dedicated my vacations to yoga and meditation retreats where I felt the first stirrings of faith and hope, of peace and joy. I wished these things for everyone else—and now, I wished them for my friend and her brother.

He had completed the first four rounds of chemotherapy and was to undergo a follow-up scan to determine if the treatment was working. If not— if the tumor had grown or had continued to spread—it meant moving onto risky experimental treatments or giving up altogether.

So, I did what I could. I got in touch with four of the holiest women I know and asked them to do the praying. At 10 o'clock in the morning, as my friend's brother was wheeled into the scanner, they took to their knees in church, while I sat cross-legged on a rock in my garden and relaxed into my meditation practice. I set an intention for him—for comfort and strength, for solace and surrender, for healing.

Taking a few slow, deep breaths, I released the growing tension in my belly and throat, and let go of the customary misgivings and preferred expectations that I had cultivated my entire life . . . and I waited . . .

. . . and then . . . fireworks . . . a grand cosmic light show.

Shower after shower of glittering white light filled my heart and burst forth, the sparks fading away as they fell, tinkling like chimes in the wind until nothing remained but silence.

I somehow knew . . . I just knew . . . that each fading ember was a dying cancer cell.

I matched this awareness by imagining what this light show might look like on a CT scan. A short circuit? Electrical interference of some sort?

Sinking deeper into the peace of this vision, I smiled to think of the chaos that would follow when the doctor, in his excitement, called his colleagues over to view the scans, all of them stunned, baffled, mystified.

A few days later, my friend called to share the scan results. My throat tightened and my heart raced as I steeled myself for bad news.

"It's gone," she said in a slow, steady voice.

"Wait. What?"

"It's gone, Janet. The liver is clear. There is no sign of cancer."

A tidal wave of relief and gratitude washed over me.

"The doctors don't know what to make of it. They've never seen anything like it. It's a miracle."

My friend attributed the outcome to all the prayers that had been lifted heavenward for months. My first vote, as a physician, would be for the efficacy of modern chemotherapy. As a woman of science, I'm also open to the possibility that our noble quantum universe had something to do with it, that our thoughts can shape our reality.

Yet after my meditation experience that day, I knew that some other benevolent force was at work. Call it synchronicity, or destiny, or just plain good luck . . . but then, who would I thank for it? The stars? Some force field? The rhythm of the tides?

Someone should be thanked for it. If God had a hand in it, He should be thanked. So, maybe I should surrender and return to prayer. I don't have a definitive answer but one thing seems certain: We witnessed a mystery . . . or perhaps we created one.

Janet Cincotta, M.D.

THE HIGH COUNCIL

*S*itting half-lotus on a yoga mat atop a boulder in my backyard, the soft summer breeze and early morning sun caressed my skin and bathed my face. As soft, ethereal music streamed through my headset, my eyes softly closed. Beautiful colors and shapes began to swirl in my inner vision. I slowly sank into a meditative state with the joyful singsong of birds complementing the music in my headset.

Most of my meditations never progress beyond just sitting quietly, allowing the energies of earth and sky to fill and renew me. Occasionally, a spirit will approach me in a meditation. When this occurs, I've developed the habit of asking, *Who is your Lord?* based on a passage in Paul's First Letter to the Corinthians.

Having grown up Christian and spending years in the church and Bible studies, I had committed myself to following Jesus. He had appeared to me in a few vivid dreams before I had a profound spiritual awakening. Due to my religious background, when my spiritual senses were heightened following that awakening, I remained vigilant that only messengers from God could come to me in my meditations.

This day, as I sat watching the kaleidoscope of colors and shapes swirling around me behind my closed eyes, the scene changed to a grassy bluff with a vivid blue sky and fluffy white clouds sweeping along in the breeze. The tall grass was moving in waves, as if dancing in the wind on angels' wings.

Ahead of me was a circle of 24 highly respected elders sitting in tall, straight-backed wooden chairs, and wearing simple white robes with sashes or cloaks of various textures and colors. Twelve of them on the left side of the circle—all weathered and wise with gray beards, although vibrant and full of vigor—exhibited an air of leadership. I understood that they represented the 12 tribes of Judah. They leaned over the armrests of their chairs toward one another, chatting and laughing amicably.

The remaining 12 on the right side appeared younger, although they, too, had beards and emitted an energy of importance. They seemed honored and grateful to be in this place. As I observed them, I realized that I was gazing upon the 12 disciples of Jesus.

A slim, honey-brown-skinned woman dressed in a sapphire-blue robe walked up to the elders and spoke with each one, attentively asking if they needed anything. She then approached me at the perimeter of the circle.

Who is your Lord? I asked.

Yeshua is my Lord, she responded without hesitation.

I recognized the name Yeshua as the Hebrew or Aramaic version of Jesus.

And who are you, if I may ask?

Of course. I am Zipporah. She smiled warmly at me, as if she were a neighbor introducing herself. The breeze blew her long, dark hair softly away from her sun-kissed face. I immediately thought of the biblical Zipporah, daughter of the Midianite priest Jethro, and wife of Moses.

Aren't you Moses' wife?

Yes, that is true.

Then how can it be that Yeshua is your Lord? You lived many centuries before he was born.

Oh! We all know him here. He is highly regarded. Would you like to see him?

The shock was surely visible on my face.

Come, Stacy. She took my hand and led me into the center of the circle, where I noticed an ornate chair of intricately carved wood. The 12 tribal leaders of Judah were circled behind it, as if providing a foundation, and the 12 disciples faced it.

Seated on the regal chair was my beloved Jesus! Every detail captivated me—his glowing bronze skin, dark hair, radiant white robe, and oh . . . his eyes, which penetrated my soul. The gentleness and compassion that he exuded overwhelmed me and caught my breath.

Motioning for me to approach, I rushed forward and fell at his feet, love bursting from every fiber of my being. With tears streaming, and kissing his feet, he lifted me up, and I sat on his knee like a small child.

The love I felt in that moment was so deep, pure, and powerful that it obliterated everything else. I only wanted to sit with him, lost in his gaze, listening to his voice.

You have come so far, he affirmed. *It is time for you to look into seminary.*

As I completed the meditation, I felt only peace and gratitude for these moments with Jesus.

I had not really thought about seminary prior to that meditation. When I went through confirmation in the church, I had a fleeting idea that perhaps I could be a minister, but was told women weren't permitted to do that, so I didn't give it further consideration.

It took several more urgings from Jesus for me to look into seminary, but Jesus' personal message that day gave me the direction and purpose I had been searching for following my awakening. Now an ordained interfaith minister, I am faithfully following where Jesus has led me to this day.

Rev. Dr. Stacy Goforth

MY QUEST FOR WORLD PEACE

*W*hile most people view me as a sunny optimist who loves to laugh, I've battled depression since the tender age of 11.

Landing a successful career at Microsoft in my twenties did nothing to alleviate my chronic depression; it simply introduced another disruptive bedfellow named anxiety. I had heard that meditation could help with this, but like many high-tech employees, I wasn't making time to learn how to meditate.

That all changed when 9/11 rocked the world and my relationship with it. The divisive aftermath of this tragic event shook me awake to the massive conflict and suffering of our shared human experience. Newly aware of my previous complacency, I made a vow that day to do my part and devote my life to bringing more peace and compassion to the planet. I saw meditation as a way to face the madness of my monkey mind and address the blind spots that enabled me to turn a blind eye to our collective human suffering—including my own.

Just days after 9/11, I gave notice and left the security of corporate America to explore a new way of life and hopefully heal. I took a Vipassana meditation course as my first commitment towards inner peace. The instructor gave me three vital words that became the cornerstone of my practice: relax, observe, allow. With these words, I learned how to become an observer of my mind and identify the negative thinking that often fuels mental health challenges. Observing was one thing, but relaxing and allowing? Not so much. I didn't know how to stop judging and reacting, which made life overly dramatic for me and those around me. I secretly hated myself for this and desperately wanted to change.

While I was determined to deconstruct the defensive ego that I had painstakingly built over years of climbing the corporate ladder, my mind wanted to do anything but meditate. As days, weeks, and months passed, I refused to give up, even repeating the course three times before mindfulness became my regular practice. What kept me on the cushion was reminding myself that this was bigger than me; it was about bringing more peace and compassion to the world.

One day, while meditating in my houseboat on Lake Union in Seattle, an energy suddenly enveloped and expanded inside of me until every cell in my body was vibrating. I felt as if my body had previously been a deflated balloon, and now something was blowing fresh air into me so I could expand and fully live as who I was meant to be.

As this mysterious force washed over me, my head tilted back, and my mouth opened involuntarily towards the ceiling as if to receive this energy from above. My body began rocking in a circular motion independent of my control. Tears streamed down my face as I experienced this reunion with something that felt beyond me but was simultaneously part of me. In this space, there was no depression, no anxiety, no self-loathing. I felt only at home and at peace.

What was this energy? I wondered. Whatever it was, it felt blissful and benevolent, and I wanted more of it.

After sitting in meditation for a while, my neck started to hurt, so I straightened my posture. The rocking stopped, and the ecstatic experience was over. Disappointment and confusion returned almost immediately.

"God, was that you? What am I supposed to do now?" I asked out loud.

Hoping for an answer, I yelled the question this time. "GOD, WAS THAT YOU? WHAT AM I SUPPOSED TO DO NOW?"

Realizing that I was alone in my houseboat, I felt foolish expecting a response. Resigned that I wouldn't get one, I retrieved a mug of tea that I had made before settling in and felt nudged to read the message on the teabag.

Live light. Travel light. Spread the light. Be the light.

What? Was this trivial teabag message God's response to my question? Was being the light my life's mission? How does that translate to bringing more peace and compassion to the planet? How does it translate into a career? The recovering Type A personality in me wanted to know.

Even without an answer, I emerged from that meditation a changed person.

Similar experiences continued sporadically in the months that followed, and I often felt this same expansive energy filling me during meditation. If this was indeed God, it was too big for me to conceptualize. So, I named the power Big Em, as it felt like me, only more divine. At times, the energy of Big Em hugged my body, like putting on a favorite old shirt. Without any frame of reference, I began describing her as my higher self, my soul. When she visited, she seemed to replenish me.

Feeling this familiar yet inexplicable energy in meditation was already strange enough when things took an extraordinary turn. One day, as I sat on my cushion, another distinct yet familiar presence was revealed—almost like bumping into an old friend in the grocery store. But it wasn't Big Em this time. It was Jesus Christ!

Having been raised in the Catholic faith, my personal Jesus appeared in the form I most recognized: white robe, shoulder-length dark hair, a compassionate yet determined expression on his face. I sobbed uncontrollably in his presence, my body convulsing with joy as this unexpected reunion occurred vividly in my mind's eye.

The Jesus visits continued, and with them came specific guidance about actions I could take to be an ambassador of peace in my unique way, including volunteer work with the United States Department of Peace initiative. When I felt uncertain or unqualified to fly to Washington D.C. and lobby the U.S. Congress on behalf of peace, Jesus came to me in meditation. As if reading my thoughts, he showed me a vision of my tiny human body standing outside of the U.S. Capitol. When I built my case for smallness and unworthiness, Jesus didn't reply. Instead, he projected an image of my body gradually growing in volume until I was twice the size of the Capitol building. This inspired me to recognize that when I stepped fully into the soul of Big Em, I was more than large enough to handle the task at hand. I was soon on an airplane to Washington, D.C.

In one incredibly intense visual encounter, Jesus walked with me down a hallway until we came upon a door. When he reached to open it, enormous billows of fire gushed out, threatening to burn us. Each consecutive time Jesus attempted to open the door, red flames emerged, leaving no safe way to enter the room. After the third attempt, Jesus calmly closed the door and looked at me.

That uncontrolled heat is your anger. It's impossible to get any new information to you when you are so angry, Jesus said. *Once you are able to address your rage, we can resume.* With that, he vanished.

I didn't consider myself an angry person; but, upon reflection, I knew Jesus was right. My defensive anger was just below the surface of my niceness, waiting to violently engulf me—and anyone close to me—in a wave of searing hot flames.

The recognition of my internal rage led me to do more inner work, for which I sought counseling support. I spent time alone and in therapy in extreme discomfort . . . naming, feeling, and being with the unhealed traumas in me that were the cause of my repressed anger, and likely, depression. After significant time and healing, Jesus returned to my meditations, and we easily walked through the once fiery door.

Feeling grateful and blessed that I decided to trade in my high-tech career for a meditation cushion, I've continued my practice over the years. Meditation has given me greater mental health, and the confidence to fulfill my post-9/11 commitment to bring more peace and compassion to the planet, knowing that my outward work for peace is guided by the Prince of Peace.

Emily Hine

THE MONKEY WITH THE GOLDEN KEY

*R*efreshing, salty air filled my lungs as I inhaled several satisfying, deep breaths. My tension melted away with every exhale, relieving my exhausted body. Gently opening my eyes, I admired the unoccupied Malibu Beach surrounding me and the serenity of the majestic Pacific Ocean. Supported by my favorite blue beach chair and shaded with a multicolored umbrella, I surrendered my toes into the sand and welcomed the invigorating, foamy waves as they swept over my feet.

On this day, I had driven an hour from my Los Feliz home on the east side of Los Angeles to find clarity, centeredness, and a sense of direction after a devastating life crisis. Frustration, confusion, and sadness filled me all at once. I had been feeling unsupported by loved ones and furious at my spiritual mentors.

Lonesomeness and abandonment had seeped deeply into my consciousness, causing me to question my life choices, including leaving my secure Canadian lifestyle two years prior. Bridging the contemporary with the spiritual was a trek that I had signed up for, but I did not realize how difficult the journey would be.

My daily ritual upon waking—a combination of pranayama, japa, journaling, and a silent meditation—often offered me a boost and brought coherence to my heart and mind. I could not detach, however, from the tyranny of my monkey mind. My thoughts would continuously walk a line of victimhood rather than victory.

Earlier that morning, sitting in front of my deity-heavy altar hadn't produced favorable results, as it often does. The piercing silence to my request for direction and reprieve infuriated me. So, I charged off to the consecrated land of Malibu, which has an ambiance that is perfect for rejuvenation. I often wondered, looking into the ocean, if history and science were accurate in that all life started in the cavernous sea, and that perhaps deep within our subconscious, we can feel the pull of our distant ancestors. The waters always pulled me in with great awe and wonder.

Indigenous Californians known as the Chumash Indians had lived in the region for centuries, performing many sacred rituals and ceremonies. The Self Realization Fellowship Lake Shrine, founded by my great-granduncle, Paramahansa Yogananda, was housed only a few miles from this spot, off the Pacific Coast Highway. This peaceful area felt like my home, a safe haven, having discovered this benevolent portal to clarity and healing only a year earlier.

As I continued to take in the magnificence of the swaying ocean, my heart softened to the harmonies of the incoming waves. Soon I closed my eyes again, focusing on my third eye. Within a minute, my physical senses shut down and I entered into a portal of Divine light.

Dropping into a mysterious and timeless domain, I survey the inner terrain and realize that I'm in an eclectic, dim-lit chamber. The walls are made of stone and white-washed wood with many tapestries hanging from metal posts. A flaming fireplace illuminates two high-backed oak thrones encircled by beeswax candles in the center of the room. The air carries a sweet, woody, citric scent, like that in an ashram, temple, or church.

Unexpectedly, a soft yet authoritative voice shouts from the direction of the oak chairs.

Rajprem! Shah! Sujon! Come! she exclaims.

Taking several cautious steps toward the throne, I am stunned by the presence of a beautiful woman sitting delicately on the throne. The fire's glow highlights her porcelain skin, large crystal-green eyes, flowing chestnut hair, and alluring smile. Her silky white robe covers her dainty yet elegant structure. She's wearing a daisy-flowered crown, and purple-blue gems dance around her wrists and neck, accented with *rudhraksha* seeds.

Her grace and beauty mesmerize me. I have never felt the quality of love she is emanating. My entire being wants to dance to her rhythms, embrace her with the deepest adoration, and dive passionately into her soul. She beams reverence from every pore of her body. There is an undeniable familiarity that I cannot decipher. Is this my mother, sister, or lover? Is she a goddess, priestess, or simply a messenger of God?

This beatific being directs me to sit in the opposite throne, speaking in a tongue that I understand yet sounds so foreign.

I am Sophia, she says, and proceeds to give me mind-blowing messages.

I gape at her presence, blown away by her celestial magnetism, and I hang on every word she utters. After some time, Sophia reveals herself to be one of my guardian angels.

We've had many lifetimes together not only on this planet, but worlds beyond this Milky Way, she imparts.

For the duration of our short-lived conversation, Sophia offers revitalizing grace and wise words. Her exquisite visage shifts every now and then. Her eyes change colors, shapes, and sizes while describing our various past interactions.

Eventually, in my mind's eye, Sophia magically produces a cherry-red wooden box with two swans carved on the top. Her ethereal hands open the regal box in front of me, exposing a shiny golden skeleton key with a crowned bow handle. Sophia unravels the significance of the specially encased gift she is passing onto me.

Allow this key to melt into your hand. The keyhole sits in your heart. It will unlock the messages encoded in your soul to guide you on your earth-born path. When you need guidance, place your palm over your heart. Remember, you are never alone on your journey.

I retrieve the special endowment from the box and place it in my right palm. Within seconds, the heavy key melts into my hand, sending shivers up my spine. The form becomes formless. As the key disappears, so does Sophia.

After what seemed like eternity, I found myself in my beach chair again. Opening my eyes, I realized that I was once again in front of the grey-blue waters. It took me a couple of minutes to retrieve my senses and fall completely back into my physical body.

My being felt effervescent and light as I recalled my trek to the cosmic world. This auspicious meditation catapulted my energies to new heights. Allowing myself to visit the silence brought about a miraculous reward. Though I didn't have specific answers to my queries, I possessed hope, optimism, and grand support. I realized that my destiny was sitting in my hands and in my heart.

After settling back into reality, I decided to walk the beach to ground into my body. Everything looked crystal clear and breathtaking as I rose from my chair. My fresh eyes took in the majestic Santa Monica mountains, white seagulls squawking, sunbathers on the beach, and the inviting Malibu Pier ahead. I walked along the shore's edge, touching the water to clean off my sandy feet.

As I sauntered closer to the pier, I noticed two young men walking towards me having an animated conversation. As they drew near, I couldn't believe my eyes. One of the guys was wearing a white T-shirt with a cartoon monkey holding a key in the very same shape as the one I had just seen in my meditative vision.

To me, it was Sophia sending me a confirmation of our conversation and Divine attunement. I shook my head and felt a colossal grin form on my face as I passed the two unassuming individuals.

"Sophia!" I screamed out, as my heart exploded with sheer joy.

Sujon Datta

DOUBTING THOMAS

I am a soul. I am other than this body.

Experimenting with this thought while seated, rooted to the floor, in meditation, I sincerely try to make a connection with the energy of the Supreme Soul. Unexpectedly, from the forehead of the senior yogi guiding the meditation, a laser beam of light extends out and reaches mine. The light trickles into my consciousness like red-yellow living lava. As it flows warmly and tenderly, the light fills all the familiar spaces within myself and reveals new layers, as well.

Involved in this experience and also the watcher; I am observing even while surrendering to this feeling of pure love and bliss that goes far beyond anything I could have imagined.

There is no resistance as the waves overtake me, rendering my logic obsolete. As the ecstasy increases, I see—for my eyes remain open—wires of light shooting out from my being in all directions.

When the intensity subsides, I try to make sense of it, feeling that only God knows me beyond my doubts, and sees that I could not get to this place through sound or words. He came . . . entering quietly, gently, then deeply . . . . reminding me of a commitment my soul made many lifetimes ago.

My heart capitulates, and in this moment, I am lost to the world and, at the same time, finally found.

Sister Veronica

MOVING FROM WOUNDOLOGY
TO WHOLENESS

*C*an a five-year-old have a soul calling? At that tender age, I felt different and had a knowing that I am here as a voice for the world. But as separation and abandonment started to become evident with people whom I depended on as a young person, so did my separation from my true self.

Who wants to be different anyway? I would ask God. *It's too complicated, lonely, and painful.* So, I closed the door and kept my true self and innate spiritual gifts in the closet.

For the next 15 years, during the 1960s and 1970s, as the external divide deepened, so did the spiritual waters of my soul. I would turn to alcohol, be removed from many wrecked vehicles, and picked up from jail by my father. The rivers of my life that previously embraced the nectar of my Divine connection became the alcohol I poured into my body in any form I could find. My belief was, *I am too different and I don't want to be here.* My heart had hardened and I was losing my life right before my eyes.

At some point, I had enough hope to begin longing for the next chapter in my life, so my prayer changed to: "I seek wholeness rather than brokenness. I want to live fully."

This led me to meditate and spend time in silence. Sobriety certainly helped support my inner growth and self-esteem.

My new process slowly became, "meditate, activate, rejuvenate, and integrate." It opened a clarity within my soul, eased my over-analytical mind, and enabled me to simply be comfortable with nothingness. I chose my style of meditation according to what was called for in the moment.

When I was in my fifties, feeling healthier than ever, I was excited to travel to Brazil to work with healers and unravel new layers of my soul. Imagine my surprise when the healer, who is a psychic surgeon, said to me, "You need an operation."

Well, I was speechless because I'd just had a physical with my medical doctor and I didn't know that anything was wrong with me.

My friend, who accompanied me on the trip, said, "It's not what's wrong with you, Temple; it's what's right with you."

She planted a seed within me that I will take to my last breath. I am not broken, nor do I have anything wrong with me. The core of my soul is whole, it is holy, and it is well.

While in Brazil, I meditated frequently and one day after an energy healing, I returned to my *pasada* to sit in silence for the next 24 hours. Construction was happening nearby and the noise was extremely distracting. In spite of that, I succumbed to a deep sleep then was promptly awakened by a strong tap on my shoulder.

You have always been a healer, a voice said to me.

In my semi-awakened dream state, I was shown a movie of when I was 20 years old and working in a large corporation. A co-worker had severely cut his arm and was bleeding profusely. In my innocence, I spontaneously ran over to him, put my hand on his arm and began to run healing energy onto his arm. The bleeding immediately stopped. I don't know who was the most shocked—the injured man or me.

As this dream reflection of my life as a young healer continued, the construction noise in the background became unbearably loud, taking me out of my meditative state. I got up and walked to the sliding glass door, and yelled down to the workers. Since they spoke only Portuguese, I used my hands to indicate that they needed to cease the noise, as guests like me needed quiet.

They understood what I was communicating and gave me a gesture expressing their apologies. Seconds later, another man walked into the group of workers, seemingly out of nowhere. His arm was wrapped in a bandage. He held up his injured arm and pointed it at me. Needless to say, I got the message.

This mystical experience of meditation changed me at a deep level. I clearly saw how current, future, and past time are all one. It has awakened me to a multidimensional reality of the soul. After that day of meditation in Brazil, I immediately integrated my God-given gifts as a healer and have never looked back.

Moving forward from woundology to wholeness, I shifted the beliefs I had about myself, others, and the world we share. I understood that because of my early conditioning and feeling internally divided, on occasion I saw myself as broken and the world as needing to be fixed.

Finally growing up and into my real self, I moved energetically from misfit to mystic, fully stepping into my soul mission. I am not broken. The world is not broken. We are whole, holy, and complete.

Rev. Temple Hayes

WHEN MEDITATION FOUND ME

*H*ow do you describe grace when it is gifted to you in the space of silence?

The year was 1990, and outward appearances would suggest that I was better than fine. Studying as a doctoral student at a state university and preparing to write my dissertation, I was immersed in exciting research; and with a passion for teaching undergraduate students, a dedicated career in academia was ahead of me. Rounding out my blessings was a strong social circle and supportive family.

Yet, I was adrift. Newly out of a relationship with a man I deeply loved, I was navigating the turbulent waters of loss and grief without a compass. The end of this relationship was bittersweet, as it was not due to an absence of love, but rather the realization that we were on two different paths and needed to forge forward without each other. There was no one to blame.

This was my first time sailing these emotional waters and, at times, it felt like I was drowning in pain. One afternoon, I was drawn to a particular book on my bookshelf. When I pulled it down, a faded and tattered pamphlet fell out, titled, *Introduction to Meditation*. I must have tucked it into the book at some point, although I didn't remember when.

My emotional pain was so intense that I would have done anything for relief, so I took this as a sign. Sinking to the floor, I began to read the pamphlet: *Sit comfortably and quietly. Close your eyes. Focus on the breath. When the mind wanders, gently guide it back to the breath.*

I decided to give it a try. The sunlight at that time of day was shimmering through the branches and leaves of a tree that shrouded my small porch. I followed the instructions and settled in.

Right away, I feel the depth and length of my exhalations calming some part of me that had been in utter chaos. My muscles, tissues, and even my bones, begin to surrender as I continue to sit quietly. With the faint sensation of the sun on my face, I have a strong sense that I've stumbled upon something incredibly merciful and benevolent.

A mystical vision begins to form in which I see myself walking along a long, dirt path in the direction of what I know, at a cellular level, is the Divine. When I reach the Divine, I am completely engulfed, fully held, and cradled by what I know to be God. Although I have experienced many acts of grace in my life, this direct experience of God touches into an abiding sense of peace that I never knew existed. I allow myself to fully bask in this sanctuary of silent peace.

Several important insights come to me. First, I realize that the depth of my emotional grief is equal to the depth of my love. Although my suffering is painful, I am able, in these moments, to somehow find solace in the knowledge that I have loved so deeply and that physical separation from another soul can neither erase how meaningful our relationship was nor diminish the love and respect we have for each other.

The quiet helps me to see that while the form of a relationship often changes, the love that is felt and shared does not. As I relax deeper into the presence of God, I realize that Divine Love is teaching me about human love.

Awestruck by the grace being bestowed upon me, I begin to understand how reticent I'd been to feeling loss, and that my resistance to grieving is a big part of my emotional suffering and pain. Sitting quietly in meditation, the silence is a balm that allows me to soften the defenses I had created against grief. I close the meditation, transformed.

Dr. Christine E. Kiesinger

FROM AN X TO A HEART

*D*riving to the airport for a trip to India, I noticed a simple yard sign for an open house at a local school called St. Xavier High School, or St. X. Although my teenage son was perfectly happy with his current school, for some reason, I felt compelled to ask my husband to take him to this event the next day.

I landed in India and went to a familiar temple for a meditation. As I sat on my favorite pillow in the temple and closed my eyes, I quickly entered a deep, silent space. Focusing on my third eye, I was transported to a place where I was able to be present in the peaceful stillness.

About an hour later, I sensed people quietly milling around in preparation for a yoga class. Feeling refreshed and calm, I suddenly had the curiosity to ask God/Source why I'd had such a strong feeling the prior day about something so seemingly mundane as a high school open house.

Opening my eyes, I looked up at the ceiling. Lo and behold, I saw something that I'd never noticed before: a huge X in the ceiling design. As I gazed at it, I had the odd sense that my son was meant to transfer to St. X.

Sure enough, as the months rolled forward, my son was awarded a large scholarship to St. X and became a student there the following school year. He loved his time at the school.

The following year, I returned to India on the very same day as the year before. As usual, I went to my favorite temple, and entered meditation in the same place where I had seen the X on the ceiling. At the close of my meditation, I looked up. Alas, the X was not there; in its place was a heart.

During his first year at St. X, my son's student mentor happened to be a young man who was applying for the United States Military Academy at West Point. He made quite an impression on my son. We later learned that this man was accepted to West Point and had shared the process as part of the mentoring process.

Around the time my son was a junior at St. X, I learned about a summer program at West Point Academy. This immediately peaked my son's interest, so he applied for the summer program.

"I just know this is the place for me," he shared. "I'm sure this is where I want to go for college."

As part of the submissions process, he needed to secure a nomination from a congressman or senator. We soon learned that our local congressman was a graduate of St. X High School. Upon reviewing my son's academic records, he gave him a glowing nomination to all of the service academies. We were so grateful!

My son was accepted to West Point Academy and has begun what he knows in his heart is the right career for him.

Dr. Ann Dinan

FREE IN THE SPIRIT

On a warm August evening under the light of full moon, I prepared a special place in my backyard for a meditation in nature. I created an altar of white flowers and white candles on a white-cloth-covered table and poured a libation of purified water into crystal stemware.

In the stillness, I heard the sound of a sweet voice that whispered to me even before I sat down. The voice guided me to pay close attention to every part of this evening's experience and listen from my inner knowing. It also invited me to open up my senses and not be afraid. I wondered what experience I was opening up to, but recognized that Spirit was guiding me in a different way tonight.

Facing the full moon and the mysterious clouds that hovered above the Organ Mountains in New Mexico, I placed my hands in my lap, said words of prayer, took three deep breaths then entered meditation. Immediately, I felt the physical presence of something greater—a vibration that flowed in and through me from my head to my feet and back again. At the same time, a beam of light seemed to surround me. My heart space was full with a sweet, loving, gentle, and all-knowing sensation, as if my soul was connected with the Divine in a way I had not felt before.

Do not be afraid, I heard the presence whisper. *You are in your right place. I brought you here. It is time that you begin what I asked you to do.*

I blessed and accepted these words, as my eyes filled with tears. My body wanted to dance and rejoice at such a clear message, but my soul invited me to *be still and know.*

Remaining in meditation for about an hour, I was between worlds, a place where time stands still. When the meditation felt complete, I blew out the candles, remembering the words of a song I sang with the Agape Choir: "I am free in the Spirit. Yes, I'm only here for God."

That evening, I rested well as my soul was truly satisfied. The next morning, I announced the opening of my spiritual center, Inspirational Ministries.

Our community celebrates the principles of love, peace, joy, prosperity, inclusivity, and dignity. Each Sunday, our services begin with honoring and greeting the land and peoples of the Pueblo and Apache tribes, Navajo Nation, the Mescalero Apache, and Piro-Manso-Tiwa tribes of New Mexico. We celebrate the Anasazi, the original people of this continent, and enter meditation with a quote from an indigenous leader.

I know that the Spirit of the wind, the sun, the mountains, the sky, and sea whispered to me in meditation that August evening and continues to bless our community to this day.

Rev. Carolyn Wilkins

THE UNIVERSE IS WITHIN YOU

*M*y life had fallen apart, upending any sense of security I'd ever known. In the 18 months since I met my guru, my marriage had caved in, leaving me a single mother of a three-year-old.

Money was tight as I job searched and completed graduate school, and we moved to another town 100 miles away so I could find work. My usually generous parents offered no help because after my guru had given me the name Kanu, they were convinced I'd joined a cult and that my life—as they knew me—was over.

In the summer of 1977, I managed to drive myself and my young son in an old VW van from Florida to upstate New York and park it with friends outside the ashram. Fortunately, I was able to get food assistance from the state. Spending a precious $75 of our little reserves on a two-day meditation intensive with my guru seemed extravagant, yet I felt compelled to do it.

Intensives consisted of long periods of meditation that included *shaktipat*, a transmission of kundalini energy from guru to disciple that begins the mystical spiritual journey of energy in the subtle body, from the base of the spine to the crown of the head. It is given through a mantra, a touch, a thought, or a look.

I was compelled to be at this intensive because of the profound *shaktipat* awakening I had when I first met my guru. At that time, during a meditation, I had so profound of an awakening that I was willing to do whatever it took to get more of that. I experienced myself as nothing but pure consciousness . . . a light of a thousand suns with no body and no name . . . just pure, pulsating energy. That lasted for nearly 90 minutes.

Now, sitting at the back of the meditation hall in upstate New York with about 800 other people, I watched our guru on a small stage upfront. After seeking spirituality for seven years and even receiving Kriya Yoga initiation on another path, I'd finally found what I thought was my soul's home. Ahhh . . . appreciation.

But by the start of the afternoon session, I was feeling just the opposite. When the next meditation began, my mind seemed to go crazy, like it was having a one-way argument with my guru, blaming him for how my life had completely fallen apart.

I cried hysterically—ranted, really—that if he was for real, he should come over to where I was sitting and show me. I projected everything onto him—the broken marriage, no job, no money, my parents disowning me. It was all his fault that I was out on my own with no life raft. Was I being duped into a cult after all? How could he do this to me? What did I ever do wrong to warrant such punishment?

After about 40 minutes of this internal argument, I began to threaten him. *If you don't come over here right now and prove to me you are for real, I am never coming back.*

When my internal raving was at its height, I felt an impulse to stand up. Once I did, a subtle energy began to pull me forward to where he was sitting on stage. Suddenly, I was 10 feet away from him, just staring at him. He never opened his eyes to acknowledge me. Instead, from a lotus pose, he stretched out his legs so I could see the bottoms of his feet.

Rather than seeing the soles of his feet, however, what I saw were scenes of the universe in his feet. With my eyes open, I could see cities and forests and oceans and moving throngs of people in a 3D kaleidoscope of mountains, rivers, and sky, everything dynamically moving and changing. The infinite vastness and beauty of it all mesmerized me.

After an eternity, which was probably two or three minutes, I closed my eyes to try and hold the vision. I heard the guru's voice inside my head, as clear as if he were whispering into my ear, *You see? I am giving you the universe and you are upset by losing your small, little life?*

The grace of his words penetrated my heart so deeply that all I could do was bow my head and weep . . . this time, powerful tears of gratitude.

In that moment, I knew that I was so much more than my own little life. I am a rebellious expression of the Divine in human form.

Kanu Kogod, Ph.D.

SURRENDER

*N*owhere to go . . . nothing to do . . . simply relaxing and drinking in the sound of the sea, the warm sunshine, the gentle caress of the breeze, and the exotic, sweet-spicy fragrance of climbing jasmine. At home by the sea in Madras, India, I was relaxing over breakfast with two American friends who had been living in India for a number of years. Krishna had adopted the life of a sadhu and Richard was a gifted shiatsu therapist with psychic abilities.

Both are devotees of the spiritual organization Radha Soami and, as such, they would customarily sit in meditation every morning for two to three hours. I had been meditating for several years and was on the verge of giving up, as reaching that pure state of stillness seemed unattainable. I was lucky to last 20 minutes, let alone three hours!

That morning during my friends' visit, I went about my daily ritual of cooking a huge stack of pancakes for everyone. We enjoyed our breakfast and sat in companionable silence on the front veranda.

Richard was to my left and Krishna was sitting opposite me. As I gazed at him in deep contemplation, I felt a flood of warmth and love for this gentle man with his huge compassionate and loving heart, and pure simplicity. As a sadhu, he had renounced all worldly possessions; everything he owned fit in one cloth shoulder bag. His eyes were all seeing and knowing, like two deep pools of love and wisdom.

Unlike the fidgetiness I typically experienced in meditation, maintaining eye contact with him seemed effortless as I surrendered into the depths. We sat together for an undetermined time—actually, it felt as though time had stopped.

Spontaneously, I felt a powerful rush of energy rise from the base of my spine as my entire body began to tingle and vibrate. A burning sensation at the base of my skull became stronger and stronger, to the point where the pressure and heat were almost unbearable.

Richard got up and stood behind me, and with gentle pressure, helped move the energy block. After a few minutes, the burning ceased, and energy shot up to the crown of my head. All thought stopped as I simply witnessed what was happening to me.

My perception completely shifted. Everything that usually appeared solid had dissolved into a sea of ecstatically vibrating energy with an unusual, otherworldly hue. The walls of the house, the furniture, the bushes, the trees, the sky, the air, my friends' bodies—and when I looked down, my body, too— all had dissolved into one infinite sea of shimmering, tiny energy particles. My hands felt 10 times their size, with vortices of energy whizzing clockwise in my palms—the same with my feet.

Wordlessly, the three of us got up and started to walk side by side to the beach. A vision appeared to me of the three of us in ancient times as priests and a priestess walking towards a temple by the sea. When I glanced at my companions, they both nodded in agreement.

For a long time, I'd had a fear of the ocean, of being out of my depth. So, I rarely ventured too far and tended to stay in the safety of shallow waters— afraid of the powerful waves crashing over me, or worse, sucking me under.

That fear was gone at once. Without hesitation, I threw myself into the Indian Ocean and surrendered to it, laughing ecstatically as the waves tossed me around like driftwood. We became one, the ocean and me.

Eventually and reluctantly, I left the sea's embrace and sat on the sand. Surrendering to the will of the wind, my body blew to and fro, at times almost horizontal, as if I were a blade of grass. I felt totally free and one with the elements and all of life.

This heightened sense of oneness and freedom continued for the rest of the day and into the evening. When it was time for bed, I felt too alive and energized to sleep, so I sat quietly and meditated for quite some time.

My bedroom began to fill with an unusual luminous light, and I sensed a presence that radiated profound compassion, tinged with indulgent humor. I felt warm and protected in its embrace, and for the first time in my life, truly unconditionally loved.

Athina Geordin

SAILING ABOVE THE CLOUDS

From the outside, I had an idyllic life, living on a sailboat in the beautiful Florida Keys, with a great-paying job that allowed me to work from the boat. I was surrounded by sunshine, beauty, nature, and dolphins. I had a devoted husband and friends who loved me. Yet, most days, all I could do was hide below deck and sink into the darkness of Windsong's belly.

On the inside, my life was spiraling out of control. For five years, I had been suffering from chronic illness, pain, and depression. I didn't know where to turn for answers, so I ran from doctor to doctor, pumping my body full of trial medicine. All the while, my emotional health crumbled, buried underneath a pile of rubble from years of self-doubt and feelings of *I'm not good enough*. I prayed for someone or something to save me from feeling wasted away, I was swollen and in pain, unable to gather enough energy to do anything except disconnect and numb away from the magnificence of life.

One day, one of my dearest friends encouraged me to join her on a yoga and meditation retreat. It had been three months since my first surgery and I was having difficulty recuperating. The doctors were unsure why the inflammation wasn't subsiding. Desperate for healing and grasping at anything that promised relief, I said yes.

On the first day of the retreat, we entered the large tent along with about 100 students all dressed in white. I found a spot in the back of the class and placed my yoga mat on the grass. It was a balmy day and although physically drained, I promised myself that I would keep an open heart and make the most of this weekend.

The facilitators were presenting a workshop on the 15th century Sikh healer and teacher Guru Ram Das. I had picked this class because I'd fallen in love with a yoga song by Snatam Kaur, in which she chants a mantra about him. It made me curious to learn more about him.

The class began with a short yoga set and breathing exercises followed by the teacher talking about the power of mantra, chanting, and meditation. The live music was hypnotizing as she guided us into a mantra that ended in the most peaceful silence. I could feel the vibration of the music and mantra resonate through every cell of my body. Not only was this quite exhilarating, it felt as though it was softening blockages, healing my brokenness, and realigning me with an essence of life I had not felt before, like a flower discovering for the first time that it has roots planted deeply in the life-giving earth.

The more I sang, the deeper I went into meditation, as if tuning into a long-lost frequency that I somehow knew. When the music stopped and the room went silent, I took off and sailed above the clouds. The tent wasn't there anymore, my body wasn't there anymore, and all my pain was gone. My essence connected with the most amazing healing Source I'd ever felt. Its presence filled my soul.

Please help me release the lump I have in my throat every time I think about the past five years of my life, I asked.

This loving Source began to tear away the wall of pain I had built around my heart.

Please restore my health, I prayed. A feeling of immense joy and unconditional love inebriated my heart.

When the facilitator called us back from our meditation, it felt as though I had been floating in a wakeful dream . . . very aware, and oh, so alive. I felt safe and whole again.

We broke into small groups to talk about our experiences. I shared my most intimate thoughts with four strangers from around the world, baring my soul to them unencumbered by my usual feelings of lack. For the first time in my life, I felt truly heard and seen for all that I was and held as a valued soul.

This connection with the Divine stripped away the barrier that had protected me from my pain and stopped me from seeing all the things I should be grateful for. It put me back in touch with my inner guidance. I no longer felt lost, disconnected, and unsure of how to manage my life. It's like I went into that tent with no GPS, got an upgrade to my internal guidance software, and came out a more confident driver, knowing that I have a loving guide in the front passenger seat. I found the light that would guide me back home.

Carole D. Fontaine

LOVE IS A SCIENCE

*F*eeling ecstatic, I awake ready for an early morning meditation at a California farm that is home to a community of Kriya yogis. Me and a few friends, also Kriya Yoga devotees, gather for the meditation.

I feel very in tune this morning, eager to listen to my inner presence behind the curtain of my thoughts. We begin our pranayama exercises to calm the mind.

After a few minutes, my heart blossoms like a flower as it expands through my inner senses of perception. Looking upwards between my eyebrows I see a perfect white light, gently glistening and wrapping my being within it. I surrender into this bliss.

In this state, I receive a knowing: *Love is a science.*

Overjoyed to have this realization I conclude my morning meditation in absolute gratitude for who I am and what lives through my being.

The entire world glistens in a gentle light visible only through my inner eye. Beyond physical forms, it's an all-pervading layer that conveys signs and impressions that are more real than what the physical world displays.

Afterwards, in the garden with my friend John, still beholding this inner knowing and perceiving my surroundings as patterns of energy, I giggle inwardly . . . *Wow. Everything is just energy.*

As John and I begin planting new flowers, I tell him, "Love is a science."

"Oh, I don't think of love as a science," he responds. "It's more like an art. Consciousness is a science."

"No, love is a science," I say with certainty. "Look at all these plants. Love is the force that heals and lets life grow. Whatever science we perceive as human beings is from the intelligence of love."

The next morning, after experiencing another wonderful meditation of directly perceiving the Divine through my inner senses, it is time to head home. I pack my bags and bring them out to the car. Wanting to double-check that I didn't leave anything behind in the room, I head back up to do a quick scan and notice a tiny piece of paper on the floor near the door. I grab it and begin to read what's on it, a paraphrased quote from Mahatma Gandhi:

"Just as a scientist will work wonders out of various applications of the law of nature, even so a man who applies the laws of love with scientific precision can work great wonders. For the force of nonviolence is infinitely more wonderful and subtle than the material forces of nature like, for instance, electricity. The law of love is a far greater science than any modern science."

Where did this paper come from? Why is it so perfectly placed near the front door where I would see it? I hadn't shared my thoughts with anyone besides John and I knew he wouldn't put the paper in my room. In fact, I have the intuition to place the paper on the windshield of John's car.

Feeling overjoyed and awed, I go outside to look for John and find him picking flowers for the farm table.

"Do you remember when I said yesterday that love is a science?" I asked. "Yeah."

"Here. Read this." I hand John the paper with the quote.

"Wow. I need this in my life. Can I hold onto this paper?"

"Of course. I was going leave it on your windshield anyway. It's for you."

Kimia Yaqub

LIVING IT

It was an absolutely idyllic day for sailing. The warm, balmy breeze felt like silk flowing against my bikini-clad body and sun beams glistened all around, electrifying the translucent aquamarine of the Caribbean Sea.

My boyfriend, Michael, had surprised me with a long weekend on the Bahamian Island of Freeport. I had brought along a book that a friend had given me, *Autobiography of a Yogi* by Paramahansa Yogananda. As I started reading it on the plane, I couldn't put it down. All I wanted to do was delve deeper and deeper into the mind of this man who was telling his story of how he became a self-realized master.

That weekend, we set out sailing on the clear blue-green sea for a day of diving and snorkeling. The water was deep yet so clear that we could see to the bottom. Excitedly, I jumped off the side of the boat without a snorkeling mask.

After swimming around a few minutes and seeing the exquisite life beneath the surface, I realized that I'd better put on a mask before going deeper.

"Hey, would someone please throw me a mask?" I yelled out playfully to the people on board.

Seconds later, rich red blood began to permeate the pristine water around me. I was stunned. When the person onboard shot the mask at me, I caught it fine—except a metal piece on it was so sharp that it cut a formidable gouge into the pinky finger on my left hand.

As blood flowed around me in the water, a few people on the boat implored, "Get back on the boat!"

I was in shock at the sight of the blood, so my boyfriend escorted me to the boat's edge and several others pulled me up.

"Get me a towel, please, quick!" I shouted and started to sob.

Everything began to look like a weird image through a fisheye lens. People were frantically coming to my aid, causing the boat to slightly rock. Someone handed me a beach towel and I wrapped it around my hand.

Suddenly, a woman emerged and grabbed my arm.

"Step away!" she demanded to everyone.

The woman led me downstairs to the cabin and sat me down. With my head lowered, she held me lovingly then began to put me into a guided meditation to calm me. I kept my eyes closed, still holding my left arm high with the towel cushioning my injured finger.

"Imagine cool, pure water coming up through your feet and cleansing your entire body," she spoke in soothing, soft tones. "Now imagine illuminating light coming from above through your crown chakra and filling your entire body. Let's take some slow, conscious breaths together."

Following her instructions for the next 10 minutes or so, I wondered, *Who is this woman? Where did she come from? How could she have known that I was into meditation?* I had never seen her before, not even amongst the 23 other people on the sailing trip.

"Now you can open your eyes."

As soon as she spoke that, I reactively removed the towel from my finger to check my wound. The woman stared into my eyes and gave me a stern look.

"You give it lip service, but you don't live it."

What? Lip service? What does she mean?

She answered my silent question.

"Why did you have to look? Where is your faith?"

This beautiful stranger, who was really no stranger, awakened me in one unexpected moment. This was Divine Source delivering a most vital message to me.

I never asked her name or anything about her, as I didn't want to break the spell of what can only be called Divine awareness.

We slowly ascended the steps to the upper deck to sail with the rest of the group. After our excursion that day, I never saw her again . . . nor did I need to.

I eventually read the rest of Yogananda's life story, and what I found most exhilarating was when the 2,000-year-old yogi would materialize to visit him, then dematerialize once again. It was the most far-out thing I had ever heard at the time, yet I knew in my heart and soul that it was truth.

I could not and did not doubt it. Just as I knew that I could not doubt the magical synchronicity that occurred with the mysterious woman who took me under her wing that glorious day on the aquamarine sea.

Dianne Collins

A LIVING SPIRITUALITY

*B*rahma Baba passed six years before I became a student with the Brahma Kumaris. Back then, I understood, on an intellectual level, Baba's role as an instrument of God in revealing spiritual knowledge, and that he had reached the *avyakt,* or angelic state. Though he had left his physical body, he was still actively engaged with us on a subtle level.

Brahma Baba's pictures were hung in our classroom in London, where I first had contact with his presence. As I was gradually drawn to his photo and sat in front of it, I felt as if he were smiling directly and only at me. I blinked several times, thinking it was an optical illusion, but his gaze was accompanied by a feeling of joy, power, and lightness beyond the senses. It was as if I was being welcomed into this spiritual family, and could feel both Brahma Baba's and God's presence.

In November 1975, I had an opportunity to visit Madhuban, the Brahma Kumaris headquarters in Mt. Abu. In those days, Madhuban was very simple, clean, and royal, bearing witness to the example of Brahma Baba's life. Our sleeping and eating arrangements were pared down and, as a Westerner and the only foreigner, it was my first experience eating meals on the floor.

Everything was carried out in the silent remembrance of God, as if Brahma Baba were still present. I was hugely impressed by the purity of the vibration. It was not an intellectual concept; this was a living spirituality.

The day after I arrived, I meditated in what we call Baba's Room—his former bedroom converted into a meditation space with a large photo of him sitting in meditation. I had heard the expression "heart-to-heart conversation", but I never really tried having one until this moment. Entering contemplation, I started to speak from the depth of my heart about the anguish of my search and the fulfillment that I had experienced in finally arriving at my spiritual destination. As I shared from my heart, I felt the answers coming back to me . . . not only answers, but the power behind them.

The following evening, the entire teaching connected back to my heart-to-heart conversation the day before. At one point in the meeting, someone asked the question, "If we realize that we have arrived at our true destination, why are we still hanging around at the door?"

Our teacher gave the example of moths plunging into a flame. Some go straight to it, and some circle continuously without having the courage to jump into the flame. Others circle around a few times then fly away.

"What type of moth are you?" he queried.

I was certain that I wanted to be in the first category.

Returning to Baba's Room the next day, I immediately entered another heart-to-heart conversation, during which I realized that my life would be serving the world in whatever way I could. In meditation, I received a powerful spiritual current that gave me a sense of belonging. This was my place. This was my spiritual family. This was the work that I had to get involved in.

I had no idea what I would find when I got to Australia—which is where I had planned to go after my travels to India—but I now knew that I would carry that subtle presence with me.

As well, I knew that my life would never be the same, as I committed myself to the same aims that Baba had: To serve others tirelessly and in an unlimited way, to become pure through remembering God with love, to reestablish a sense of self-sovereignty, and to pave the way for a new, more elevated world.

Over the years since then, when I know that I have made a considerable effort in some aspect of my worldly work, Baba looks at me with genuine appreciation, and I hear him say, *Good work. Keep it up.*

Ken O'Donnell

SHOWERED IN DIVINE LIGHT

*M*aybe it was an irrational and impulsive decision to spend the last of my savings on this, I wondered as I ventured deep into the beauty of rural Quebec for a meditation retreat. *I've never even meditated before.*

Now here I am, about 10 days into the two-week retreat, and everyone is having big experiences, each one better than the last. Me? I'm falling asleep in meditation! Each day, I end up feeling rejected, frustrated, and unworthy.

Near the end of the retreat, as the August full moon approaches, we gather for a morning meditation to clear our heart chakras. Our instructor guides us to bring the translucent white ray of God into our bodies during the final part of the clearing.

As these words are spoken, my crown chakra begins to tingle. The white light intensifies and pours into my body. I am laying on the hardwood floor, hands and arms open, receiving this shower of magnificent light, as though on the grass in a rainstorm.

I physically cannot move . . . not even a finger . . . nor do I want to. This is pure bliss! Every fiber of my being is tingling, expanding, and allowing more light to enter, like the most intense and delightful orgasm possible. As the light continues to explode through me, I briefly feel my soul levitate out of my body.

At some point, I sense and hear others in the room beginning to stir as the bell rings, calling us for lunch. Though fully conscious and alert, I am still pinned in bliss and cannot move, so I remain on the floor in this shower of love, light, and grace.

"Are you okay?" the instructor asks. Several others gather in a circle around me.

Still vibrating so high, I can barely speak. Eventually, I open my eyes and movement slowly begins to return to my fingers, feet, and arms. More time passes before I can sit up, as my body continues to receive this Divine light. This is beyond anything I've ever experienced—joy, peace, ecstasy, wholeness, and light all at the same time.

The shower of light changes into what feels like waves washing over me. I motion with my hands for the others to move in closer. Reaching out, I grasp the hands on either side of me within our circle.

As we physically connect, another wave of light and love washes through me. It passes through my hands and around the circle to each person. Looking up, I see glowing surprise shining on their faces. We sit together for some time, connected in silence, in light, in love, and in bliss.

Eventually, we begin to make our way towards the cafeteria for our midday meal. As we walk, one woman in the circle approaches me with open arms for an apparent embrace. As she nears, I feel the energy surge through me, pushing her back approximately eight feet.

She approaches again and this time the electricity flows through my body towards her, preventing her from advancing and touching me.

"I can't even get close enough to hug you!" she responds. "The energy is so strong!"

I am in joy beyond measure as the vibration of peace settles into my heart.

Ana-La-Rai

MY FATHER'S GIFT

*T*he restaurant Delmonico's in New York City was my family business since 1926, and from the time I was a little boy, "the Delmonico way" was a part of my life. At the restaurant, I was my father's right-hand son, pitching in to do everything from cleaning ashtrays to changing light bulbs. It was expected of me, and I happily complied.

You see, my father, Mario Carlo Tucci, was larger than life—a renaissance man and consummate gentleman with a gentle heart and a voice like Pavarotti. He would set up a table at the restaurant for the homeless to eat and, in an hour's time, be dining at the same table with dignitaries, politicians, and celebrities. Babbo (Tuscan for father) taught me to live a noble life, keep my shoes clean, treat the house staff with respect, and love my family. He was grooming me to someday become the next restaurateur and keeper of the Delmonico's family legacy.

All that changed at age eight, when my father died unexpectedly. Overnight, whatever boyhood dreams I kept to myself were replaced with having to fill roles that weren't mine to fill—from father, to son, to brother, to spouse—as I stepped into my dad's shoes. For years, I felt bitter, angry, and abandoned. I wanted to know: *Babbo, why did you die? Why did you leave me? Why did you leave the family that you adored so much?*

A few years later, I was introduced to meditation when I took a yoga class and met a woman named Letty Militana. A pilot, tango dancer, and yoga teacher, she became my adopted grandmother and taught me the power of stillness.

"Your initials are OM . . . Oscar Maximilian," she'd say, pronouncing my first and middle name. "You are *ommmmm*."

At age 13, practicing meditation not only fascinated me, it softened my rage, slowly opened my heart space to love more unconditionally, and became a place where I could escape and find answers.

Yet in the back of my mind, there was always this echo of *Fuck you, why?* That expletive seemed to be more so an efficient way to explain my anger, rather than being a description of it. Grandma Letty taught me to accept all my feelings and surrender to the flow. She gave me a mantra to reinforce this: *Where I am now is exactly where I am supposed to be.*

My life continued to unfold, and in my twenties, I traveled to the Kashi Ashram in Sebastian, Florida. Ma Jaya was the guru of the ashram. Intrigued by her book, I had requested an interview with her as part of my work.

When I arrived and was ushered back to meet Ma Jaya, she said in greeting:

"So, what do you want from the guru?"

"Nothing," I simply replied.

"Finally! Somebody understands it, somebody gets it, somebody doesn't want anything from the guru," she responded. "What can I give you? Nothing. I like you."

After she shared her stories with me, I was inspired to walk the grounds of this magical, 70-plus-acre ashram. As I strolled by the trees, the river, and the lake, joy was present, as well as a great quietness, surrounded by the natural musky scents and essences of the animals and plants.

As I walked, I came upon a very old train car. How it got there, I had no idea, but I felt called to sit on the edge of this caboose. It became my refuge for the rest of the afternoon.

Relaxing into meditation, a picture began to coalesce in my head—visions of myself as a child, working at the restaurant then standing at my father's grave. At eight years old, swear words weren't in my vocabulary but I saw myself in this vision, standing at his grave, crying, and screaming, "Fuck you! Fuck you! Fuck you!" . . . and feeling the crush of his death on my life.

Staying with this vision, I felt my breath more than I ever had, inhaling, holding, and exhaling . . . inhaling, holding, and exhaling . . . the out-breaths being longer than the in-breaths . . . and on the inhale, at one moment, it was as if I were in a portal.

The whole universe shifted, including my own self-paradigm. I could see that my father's death was something very life-giving for me. I understood, for the first time, that his life at the restaurant was his life, which he had followed in his father's footsteps. My father was creating this dynasty that was my grandfather Oscar Tucci's destiny, but it wasn't *my* destiny.

Beneath my breath, I kept hearing the words, *His death gave me my life. His death gave me my life. His death gave me my life.*

Right there in that meditation, the chain and ball that bound me to my anger were released. The *fuck you* turned to *thank you.* The anger was replaced with gratitude for everything being exactly as it is supposed to be—just like Letty's mantra promised.

My heart healed as I was freed from the patterns and pathologies of my father's father to take over the restaurant. From this day forward, I could live the life of my choosing, and do what I was born to do, my soul destiny. My father's passing was his priceless gift to me to become the man who I am.

Max Tucci

INFINITE LIGHT

*H*e outstretched his hand to offer a bouquet of jasmine flowers and I came in close to take them. It was as if a magnet pulled my inner being, the soul, out of the consciousness of my body and the world around me.

It was nighttime and a group of us were outdoors in Mount Abu, Rajasthan, sitting in a circle around Brahma Baba, the founder of the Brahma Kumaris. He was sharing *drishti,* which is the practice of focusing, with eyes open, on soul consciousness and God. Everything was white and sparkling: his pristine clothes, the sweet jasmine flowers, and all else seemed to be blurred in white light.

I was totally unaware of the physical form of Brahma Baba. The place that I was carried to was one of infinite light—not like the light of the sun here in the physical dimension, but a pure, boundless light that has a special glow. It seemed to be familiar, as if I had come home. It was silent, peaceful, and very warm. Immersed in this light, I realized that what I had felt as a magnet was the Divine. My perception became one of connecting with the Divine, and understanding that I, in my infinitesimal form of light, and the Divine are the same; yet, of course, there is a difference.

Light, as I've experienced it, encompasses three different things: my experience of the self as light, the form of the Divine as light, and this infinite light that was my home. All three were different. The light of home seemed to be celestial, and golden with a tinge of red. The light of God I felt as intense yet kindly, accompanied by a sense of an eternal bond, a relationship of myself with this Divine Being. God's light was filled with unlimited, unconditional love, as though I was reuniting with someone whom I loved dearly after a long separation.

The feeling of my own light wasn't as radiant as the beauty of the light that was now reaching me; however, I sensed a transformation. It was changing something within me because of the experience of pure love and total acceptance by God. There was also a feeling of power that was filled with much compassion, and that power was also being poured into the soul. This went on for a short time, yet the experience was an infinite moment, a feeling beyond the limits of time.

Somehow, the magnetic force began to gradually reduce and I gently came back to the awareness of the physical dimension. The rich fragrance of the jasmine flowers reached my senses, and I once again was aware of holding out my hands to receive the flowers from Baba's hand. Baba continued to gaze at me, and it was clear that he understood exactly what had happened, as if he had planned this moment of intimate encounter between the Divine and me.

I sensed the other yogis around me and, while still holding my gaze, Baba asked them:

"Do you know why Baba is giving this child *drishti*?"

One of the others smiled and nodded her head in understanding of what had just happened. In this infinite moment with the Divine, a new birth had taken place and I surrendered my life to God and to serving humanity.

Sister Jayanti

THE MEDITATION THAT TAUGHT ME TO BE LOVE

*D*elighted to greet a few old friends at the Toronto Convention Center for a weekend workshop with my spiritual mentor, laughter and excitement filled the air. Taking my seat, I joined more than 200 students from all over the world who had converged to delve into and connect more deeply with the intelligence of Divine Love.

During the first morning's meditation, I followed the instructions about how to connect to Divine Love and receive a personal message. Relaxing more fully into my chair with my eyes closed, I went into the sacred space of my own heart and asked the question, *Love, what do you most want me to know today?*

After a pause, I distinctly heard in a clear, calm voice that felt like guidance from a loving parent: *Be love.*

In the span of a single heartbeat, a cascade of images appeared across my mind's eye like a series of stills from an old movie reel. The story unfolded both in a linear fashion and all at once, outside of ordinary time. I could see, hear, and feel the messages being presented. These images shifted into a video format in my mind's eye, and before I understood what was happening, I was looking down and observing myself walking up the steps leading to my daughter's front porch.

As both the observer and the observed, I saw myself looking through the glass front door at my then 15-month-old grandson, Emory. The energy of love encircled our hearts and a wide grin broke out on his face as he recognized his GiGi.

The same voice as before said, *Greet everyone with an open heart, without an agenda.*

Instantly, I recognized that this is the way I greet Emory—no expectations, no agenda, just pure love responding to love.

In a flash, I was inside the house with my beloved Emory, but I wasn't seeing him in his physical form. I looked through him into a brilliant, effervescent light at his core . . . his soul.

See the Divine essence in everyone, I heard. The truth of this resonated deep within me.

Barely processing that thought, the scene before me changed again. Emory and I were now alone in the living room, playing with building blocks. He awkwardly tossed one to me, as a toddler does, hitting me on the cheek directly under my eye. I felt only compassion and understanding, as I realized that he didn't know how to aim. He meant no harm. Again, the inner knowing came through loud and clear:

Forgive quickly, completely, unconditionally. He's a baby. He's just learning.

The scene changed once more to a darkened room where I could see only the outline of a massive door. It seemed to hang in space without support from the walls, ceiling, or floor. The door slowly opened, just a crack, and a sliver of bright, iridescent yellow light teaming with vibrant, joyful energy streamed out.

Even this tiny amount of energy overwhelmed me with a feeling of bliss I could barely comprehend. Tears streamed down my face as I heard:

You're all trying to get back here but you don't understand. You're already there. You never left the light of the All. You just have to remember.

I realized that the love I felt for Emory is but a tiny fraction of the love that is in the light of the All. This same love is not only available to each of us, it *is* us. These moments were beautiful, mesmerizing, powerful, and serene. I was speechless as the tears continued to flow . . . and then it was over.

Did that really happen? I wondered as I opened my eyes. My mind reeled as I tried to understand what had occurred. It took months to process the experience and comprehend fully this message of Divine Love.

In retrospect, before that weekend retreat, my heart had been calling me to deeper service and in prayer I had asked for specific guidance. In this meditation, my prayer had been answered. This experience filled me with gratitude and energized a new purpose in me—to do my part to teach others how to "be love" in the world . . . and more importantly, to be love myself.

Diane L. Haworth

OM SHANTI

a petite Indian sister approached out of the blue and greeted me as I stepped out of the Suzuki.

"May I help you?" she asked with a friendly smile.

"Yes, I've come for a blessing through the eyes from Dadiji Prakashmani."

A refreshing breeze blew her white cotton sari into what looked like angel wings. She reminded me of Mother Teresa of Calcutta.

"Welcome, I'm Vedantibhen. Would you mind receiving a brief introduction of our teachings before you meet Dadiji? This way, you will be more comfortable with her."

"Yes, of course." I wanted to know everything.

Vedantibhen introduced me to Jasubhen, an English-speaking sister from Zimbabwe, who led me to an outdoor lounge. A large wicker fan blew a cool breeze overhead, wafting the aromatic scent of Indian cooking into the room. My stomach rumbled, reminding me that I hadn't eaten since breakfast.

"Who are you?" Jasubhen asked once we got settled.

Unsure of her question, and after some thought, I answered, "A spirit inside a body."

Raising her eyebrows, she seemed stunned at my response. "You *know* that? Most people say, I am Deborah, or I am a nurse . . ."

"Yes. I studied for many years with a Native American medicine woman. She taught me this."

"The spirit, or soul, comes into the body through the third eye," Jasubhen went onto explain. "An infinitesimally small point of light, a star, sits right in the center of your forehead. We say the word *om* . . . meaning, 'I am a soul.' *Shanti* . . . means 'peaceful.' *Om shanti* . . . means 'I am a peaceful soul.'"

Oh, my gosh, I couldn't believe it—I'd spent a lifetime searching and trying to understand this concept of the third eye, but no one had taught me about it in this specific way. The notion of the soul entering the body through the third eye made my heart race with exhilaration, like I had found the ultimate answer.

"We teach meditation with our eyes open," Jasubhen explained. "You can meditate while you wash dishes, drive your automobile, or even while sitting comfortably in a chair. All you have to do is remember who you are—a peaceful soul. When we meditate, we connect our soul to the Supreme Soul, God the Father." She pointed to her forehead. "Let's practice together, okay?"

Jasubhen led me into this form of open-eyed meditation. Very soon, a strong tingling sensation raced up and down my spine, causing my face to pinken with joy and anticipation.

Unbeknownst to her, Jasubhen had answered my most deeply held questions in the course of five minutes . . . such as *What is the third eye? . . . How do you meditate?*

In the midst of this meditation, something awakened inside of me. My whole body trembled, and a combination of peace, joy, and exhilaration surged through me all at once. Overcome with bliss, sensations that I had never experienced tickled every whit of my being . . . then it was time to meet Dadiji, a renowned spiritual leader from northern India, and her jolly companion, Mohinibhen.

Jasubhen escorted me into a small, comfortable salon and introduced me to the two women. I noticed a sweet smell in the room, which delighted my senses.

Dadiji and I chatted for a few moments yet the words we spoke weren't as important as the vibration between us—an ambience so powerful that it was palpable in the atmosphere. It seemed to touch my skin and send shivers all over my body as I relaxed back into a state of deep meditation.

All the while, Dadiji's eyes gazed into mine, but they didn't appear to see me. Her eyes reached deep into my third eye and to my soul, and I felt it as a blessing.

I wanted to stay in her gaze forever, but soon enough, it was time to go. How long had we been here? How much time had passed? I didn't know. I didn't know anything except that I was intoxicated.

Dadiji lovingly placed a small Indian chocolate mint into my hands, still looking deeply into my eyes. Mohinibhen, with a sweet giggle, handed Dadiji a full-blooming, fragrant rose. Dadiji, in turn, bestowed it upon me. Still, those eyes stared at me.

As I exited the room, my feet felt as though they were three feet off the ground . . . my whole being was like a helium balloon floating in pure love and bliss.

With help from two of the sisters, I managed to make my way back to the Suzuki, still floating. The sweet sisters and I said our goodbyes by sharing the two words that we all understood: *om shanti.*

Deborah Lyn Thompson

SPIRIT OF THE SPRING

Someone once asked Mahatma Gandhi how many religions there are.

"In reality, there are as many religions as there are individuals," he replied.

When I heard this concept, it stayed with me, as I desperately tried to deal with my inner turmoil through meditation. I had been struggling with memories of seeing deadly violence in Makeni and a wave of horrible atrocities sweeping through Sierra Leone.

Going inward to the place of the witness, through meditation, brought temporary glimpses of peace, but for the most part, I could not understand why such suffering existed in the world. I was looking for something beyond the witness. I was looking for God, both for comfort and to understand how in the hell He or She or It could allow such wars to happen.

The Kriya Yoga tradition challenged my concept of God and offered a new one to explore. While God was beyond and part of all creation, the Divine could be worshipped in many different forms, both personal and impersonal, depending on culture and individual orientation. Impersonal aspects could be states of being such as emptiness, peace, bliss, light, or ecstasy.

I clung to Kriya Yoga methods like a life raft. They are systematic in using breath and mantras to relax the body, focus and calm the mind, and bring energy and consciousness inward. I would imagine energy being brought up the spine and focused at the spiritual eye between the eyebrows, the doorway into subtle realms of consciousness.

The spiritual eye, with its yellow outer ring, was an old friend from my childhood, as I would go to sleep looking into it. I learned in yoga that the golden ring corresponded with a frequency of vibration of energy and consciousness—that of Divine Mother, or the Holy Ghost, or Great Comforter, Om—the energy that created everything in the universe.

Inside the golden ring is a field of blue, or Christ Consciousness—the intelligence that exists in and guides the energy manifesting creation. It is the consciousness that Christ, Krishna, and other holy people embodied. In the field of blue is a white star, or Cosmic Consciousness, or God the Father, that exists beyond creation.

I added to all of this a technique that intuitively felt right: While looking at the spiritual eye, I visualize the space around me and then outward, to span all of the Washington, D.C. area, the United States, the western hemisphere, Africa and the eastern hemisphere, the Earth, solar system, and Milky Way Galaxy with billions of stars, until I can imagine billions of galaxies spinning. An effect of this visualization is that my ego is completely humbled by the overwhelming awareness of the vastness of the universe.

At some point in my meditation practice, when I reached that point of expansion while imagining billions of galaxies, I began to pray deeply for Divine Mother to come to me.

"Divine Mother, reveal yourself! Reveal yourself!" I pleaded.

A few weeks after I began calling in Divine Mother, I went on a trip to a friend's farm in Ohio. Given my monk-like habits, I was excited to stay in a small wooden hut next to a spring house and stream-fed pond. The sound of the water was soothing, and I found myself, at sunset, sitting next to the spring in silence. A friend from North Africa who was visiting the farm cautioned me, saying that spirits liked to hang out around water. His warning reminded me of the stories from Sierra Leone, yet I felt drawn to the water.

There was a peacefulness being so close to the water and the woods. The hut had very thin walls with large gaps between the slats of wood, reminding me of the houses in Sierra Leone and how nature was a part of the homes.

The first night, I meditated deeply then prayed again for Divine Mother to reveal Herself. Afterward, I drifted off to sleep and had a series of dreams of beautiful women dancing over the water. I felt almost drunk when I woke up. That entire day, I stayed near the water, listening. The second night, the same thing: more dreams and a feeling of deep peace.

On the drive home, I began to write poetry for the first time ever.

A couple weeks later, I went with two friends on a camping trip in the Shenandoah Valley near Front Royal, Virginia. As we hiked up a mountain trail, I intuitively felt a need to be alone in the solitude in nature. My friends walked ahead on the trail, respecting my wishes.

Slowing my pace, I started to bring my attention to the present moment, to my feet touching the Earth, to the feel of a slight breeze against my skin, to the sunlight shimmering through the leaves. Something big was happening, as I felt energized and aware of a presence, almost like a life force in the forest. I began to giggle, imagining a two-way communication with a tree.

Tuning into something ethereal, a door had opened . . . a veil pulled back and I was allowed to walk through. Each step was slow and intentional, taking in the panorama of vibrations . . . until I became aware of the presence getting stronger, as if moving toward me, yet arising from inside at the same time.

I started to stumble and feel lightheaded, as if intoxicated. Pausing to embrace a tree, I could feel the life force flowing down into its roots, up the trunk, out the limbs, and into the leaves. It was as if the sun was feeding the tree, and, in turn, the tree was feeding me an invisible elixir springing from within and permeating everything around me.

My friends eventually made their way back down the trail, talking away. They looked at me, laughed, and said, "We'll meet you in the parking lot."

Slowly, I followed behind them, finding it more difficult to walk. The presence was getting even stronger inside, so I decided to hurry down the trail to the car as best I could.

We drove through the mountains to a campground in the national forest. The site we chose was away from other people and close to a flowing spring. After getting the tents set up and a fire started, my friends offered to cook while I took a walk.

Feeling a need to go somewhere but not sure where, I headed into the woods and ended up in a thick briar patch. Stopping, I heard water babbling, and moved in that direction. Coming to a small waterfall, I carefully stepped on stones to cross the water then sat on a boulder along the bank.

There was the presence again, getting even stronger. I was not sure whether to get up and walk back to the campsite, or stay by the water. Holding my legs close to my chest, I placed my head on my knees and looked to the left. A few feet away, hanging on a tree limb, was a rosary with brown-and-yellow beads and a white crucifix. Shocked to see the holy image of the cross in this remote wilderness, I surrendered and opened.

Energy exploded from inside and washed through me, flooding me with an overwhelming feeling of love. My mind tried to comprehend what was happening, and then all thoughts were rinsed away. I stayed in a mode of receptivity, and experienced an indescribable flood of love.

Moans spontaneously poured forth, as my body pulsated in what felt like orgasms, one after the other, in a symphony of ecstasy. I grasped my legs tighter and squeezed. The love came from deep inside. On and on, waves of energy rose up the spine, blowing the heart open, clearing the mind, bursting through me. Several times, I gasped for air, barely able to contain the ecstasy. I held back screams, muffling the sounds in my arms.

There was a period of timelessness, as the experience went on and on. At one point, my moans turned into passionate words of deep longing, as I found myself saying, "I've missed you, I've missed you."

Tears began to flow, and a voice in my head said, *Silly you, I am always with you.*

Exhausted, spent, and energized all at once, I eventually opened my eyes to see that it was night. I fell softly asleep with the earth, the trees, the rocks, the sky, everything pulsating through me . . . and the water babbling nearby, knowing I had found my religion.

Philip M. Hellmich

A DIVINE ENCOUNTER

*a*s a child, while wishing upon a star—as children sometimes do—I wished for nothing short of the upliftment of humanity.

As an adult, I ventured off to India seeking awakening and enlightenment. During one of my many trips, I took part in a process called holotropic breathing, which quiets the mind and gives greater access to the higher realms of wisdom, insights, and spirituality. Holotropic breathing is intense and requires a great deal of energy.

So, I prepare myself . . . and begin.

After a while, I feel the energy building in my body. As I listen to the monk calling out the breathing rhythm, his voice fades into the background and my consciousness begins to expand. Calmly, I become fully aware of being in some newfound reality. I can feel and see that I am in a type of great hall and, to the left of my peripheral vision, I catch a glimpse of a tremendous white light. I want to turn fully towards the light; in fact, I literally try to turn my body so I can observe it straight on, but try as I might, I am not able to do so.

Suddenly, as I cease trying to look at the light, three figures appear before me, almost encircling me. While they are incased in pure white light and not clearly visible, I know exactly who is present. It is Jesus, Sri Amma Bhagavan, and the Buddha. Behind the Buddha is another being, whom I cannot quite make out, but I think it is Vishnu. It does not matter because I am again drawn back to the three figures in front of me, with Jesus and Sri Amma Bhagavan commanding most of my attention.

As I stand there, gazing at these holy beings wrapped in white light, I feel a tremendous, overwhelming love enfolding me, so gentle and sweet. Yet, at the same time, I have the desire to turn once again to my left and look upon the massive energy of pure light.

Jesus or Sri Amma Bhagavan —I'm not sure who—tells me that I am not able to look at the Godhead directly but that they fully embody that Light and that they are here to strengthen me, as well as remind me of my commitment and mission. They know about my childhood "Twinkle, Twinkle, Little Star" prayers for mankind and, of course, my adult ordination vows to serve humanity. They tell me of their unwavering support for my journey and that they are going to infuse me with their energy.

The most exquisite surge of powerful Divine love courses through my being as Jesus, Sri Amma Bhagavan, and the Buddha encircle and enfold me in their embrace. Warmth from this incredible white light stimulates every cell, every atom, every aspect of my body. I merge into them and they merge into me. I am energized, electrified, and infused with this Divine love from head to toe.

The three figures then turn me around and send me on my way. With their light now at my back, I walk into the darkness and I am back in my body.

Since this experience with the Godhead, I am filled to capacity with the strength and passion to complete my life journey and commitment to serving my fellow human beings. That day, drenched in the pure light of the Divine, I was given all that I will ever need.

Rev. Sylvia Sumter

DANCING WITH THE FLAME

Mum told me, almost every day, to go and sit in front of the huge temple situated at the end of our living room. As a child, I sometimes wondered why the gods had more seating space than we did, but I obediently followed Mum's instructions and spent at least five minutes every day at the temple.

It had an array of idols that Mum had collected over time from India, Kenya, the UK, and other places—short and tall, sitting and standing, made of marble, copper, and steel. She had also wedged a few pictures of our ancestors in between them for good luck.

The temple was a miniature of the real thing. Made from a mixture of marble and wood, our replica looked ornate in materials of red, green, and gold, with sandalwood garland hanging from its dome. A thick, rock-like, multicolored cushion on the floor in front of the temple is where we'd sit, lotus position, to say our prayers. In the mornings, Mum lit the diva, which is a cotton wick in oil. It stayed burning each morning until the oil ran out.

I never quite knew what to do once I landed on that rock. Mum would always tell me to say good morning to the gods, which didn't take long. To make Mum happy, I would sit a few minutes longer or until she felt that I'd had a good natter with them.

One morning, when I was around eight years old, I sat there staring at the diva flame, which was quite tall because the wick was long inside the vertical, golden metal holder. Hypnotized by the flame, it performed a dance before me, making my eyes dart back and forth ... back and forth . . . back and forth.

I could feel a gentle swaying of my body being lured deeper into the flame by the light ... or was it by the flame into the light?

I turned my focus to the tip of the flame, still moving as my eyes fixated on it. The flame appeared to detach from the wick and was now dancing in the air, all by itself. Long, thin rays of white-golden light started to emanate from the flame. I could feel them striking my face . . . not cold or hot, just gentle.

This star-ray formation began to expand until all I could see was the light. All else fell away and I was wonderstruck—not frightened, just being in pure silence with an inner feeling of *wow* . . . like jumping and screaming upon seeing fireworks, but this experience was quiet and simple, personal, and anonymous.

The light began to revolve clockwise and counter-clockwise. I closed my eyes to check if this was a figment of my imagination, but when I opened them, the image and feeling remained.

Interestingly, the light did not permeate the rest of the room. It was only around me, as if my whole aura was being held and charged by it. I was not present in my body and the rock cushion didn't feel like a rock anymore. Though not conscious of the time, this lasted for probably about 15 minutes.

What was that Light? I knew it was God . . . the real God. I mean, not one from the temple . . . but the One above. I had been calling to Him, asking what I should do while sitting on that rock. He had finally returned my phone call with a silent light show just for me, more awesome than any fireworks display could ever be.

Aruna Ladva

GOD'S LOVING VISION

*M*y friends affectionately called me *swami* because I was always trying to understand my inner world. My greatest challenge was creating a sense of self-value, as my inclination was to dance to the tune of how others saw me. If they approved of me, I was okay; but if not, my self-worth would plummet.

During my early teens, my parents sent me to confirmation classes every Sunday at the local church. After a few months, my family asked me what I had learned.

"I think I am an atheist," I said with the wry wisdom of a 12-year-old.

"Why do you think this?" they asked me.

"I cannot relate to someone who seems so judgmental and punishing."

I continued to label myself as an atheist, but was still searching. In fact, over the years, my search became stronger and stronger.

At the age of 20, I got a one-way ticket to southeast Asia and spent a few years traveling over land to Europe. Without having made a conscious decision to do so, I always found myself in religious communities. In

Malaysia, I lived with Sikhs in the Gurudwara, and stayed for a while in a Buddhist monastery on an island in the Gulf of Siam. I lived with Muslims during Ramadan and spent time where His Holiness the Dalai Lama lived in Dharamsal. Along the Himalayas is where I lived with a yogi and bathed in the river Ganges. After spending time in the great mosques of Iran and Afghanistan, I moved to Europe and lived in a Christian community in Belgium, finally settling in London.

As I traveled far and wide, I began to identify with being an agnostic. I realized that my atheism was more a rejection of religion, or the institutions that represent God, rather than God. My big question was: *If there is a God, how do you experience God?*

One day, I had just finished meditating at the Brahma Kumaris center in London and was walking down the road in a state of deep contemplation, yearning to connect with a higher power.

Suddenly, it was as if time stopped, and I became totally absorbed in Divine love. It felt like I was under a canopy of light that radiated such purity that it drenched me to my core and rekindled my soul's spark.

I became still . . . silent . . . wanting for nothing . . . absorbed in the Divine. The single thought that emerged was that I had come home, and this was where I belonged. Something shifted, and a door in my heart that had been closed for a long time swung open. This powerful love healed my sense of disconnection, and my wandering and searching felt complete.

After that experience, I yearned to sit more and more in meditation, and this sweet connection with the Divine continued to grow. Some of the meditations were profoundly intimate, as if I were an open book and the Divine knew my most private, personal thoughts and feelings.

God's loving vision touched a part of me that I had become blind to: my original self, my highest self, or perhaps I can say, my pure self. Through

His light, I could now see myself in a different light. My self-view changed from one of disrespect to one of respect, from negative to positive, from my limited physical self to my unlimited spiritual identity as a soul.

Charlie Hogg

AN ENCOUNTER WITH THE DIVINE

*G*rowing up in a town called Ilford on the eastern outskirts of London, I was a quiet, introverted child with a tendency to think deeply about life. When I was eight years old, my parents introduced me to Raja Yoga meditation by taking me with them to attend meditation classes at a nearby center. The individuals in the classes were mostly adults, some in their twilight years.

Sometimes we would have a yoga Bhatti practice, which is done to increase the power of the mind's concentration. It's like being in a meditation furnace for an hour or two, the goal being to melt away the weaknesses in the soul.

The subject of the Divine came up a lot in these classes, so I already had a lot of respect for this Being, but I had not yet experienced Him personally. In my usual meditation practice, I experienced myself as a spiritual energy, separate from my body, along with the magical feeling of peace that comes with it.

In those days of my childhood, my meditations came like waves, one after another, and it all seemed very common and normal to me. I couldn't understand what the adults were talking about when they discussed how to overcome the thoughts that come up in meditation.

One particular evening at the center, when I was 14 years old, I had a compelling experience of the Divine. The room was dimly lit and relaxing music was playing. I found a space to sit on the floor with about five others.

The meditation begins and I bring my attention to the center of my forehead. I feel myself as a soul, as a star, sitting there yet separate from my physical body. My body feels like a heavy suit of armor and I—the light, a spiritual energy—am wearing it to express myself in the world. With eyes open, I look through it as one would look through windows.

My soul, this tiny radiant star, flies upwards in a spaceship made of pure thought. I leave my body, up and away from the room, beyond into space, into another dimension made of an otherworldly, golden-reddish light.

There I stay . . . silent, serene, and very peaceful . . . as though I've reached my real home. My mind is totally still in this zone of timelessness.

Suddenly, I feel the presence of another Being, much brighter and bigger than me. His form is also that of a star, except waves of energy are pulsating from Him. As He comes near me, I feel a fountain of pure love emanating from Him. I stay under the fountain, absorbing this Divine love—comforted, reassured, cleansed, and empowered all at the same time. I am a sponge being filled up by the vibrations coming from this Divine Source . . . except He feels like a friend I've known for a very long time who has been watching me for many lifetimes . . . someone who knows me better than I know myself.

He is a Mother and Father rolled into one. I feel safe and whole in His presence, as though He is giving me back to myself. My heart is full as I experience love and power in equal measure down to my soul. In these moments, it becomes clear that I am a soul currently in a body, and that I have worn many body costumes before this one.

Unaware of how long I am in this timeless state, I return to the awareness of this world, realizing that my eyes had naturally closed during the meditation.

Slowly opening my eyes, I see the usual walls, pictures, and furniture, then look down at my hands and feet. It all seems so different, as though this is the world of shapes and sizes, colors and forms, but that world . . . my home . . . is the world of light, stillness, and silence.

Yogesh Sharda

STUMBLING INTO UNITY CONSCIOUSNESS

*T*he uncomfortable coughs of others getting settled in the drafty meditation hall echoed off the rafters. About 300 of us had gathered for a six-day silent meditation retreat. Finally starting to get my groove back after a recent divorce, I had been looking forward to immersing in these few days of peaceful quiet.

With a cozy pink pashmina around my shoulders, I am eager to begin a round of seven 45-minute sittings. As the meditations progress, the atmosphere is silent but the monologue in my restless mind grows unrelenting. I never knew a silent retreat could be this loud and I feel annoyed with myself.

After a round of meditations, it's time for the Q&A portion of the retreat with our teacher, which is the only time we're allowed to use our voices. Still feeling agitated, I find myself half-listening and half in a state of no thought.

In an instant, inexplicably, my perception shifts from being with everyone in the room to becoming the room. Every question and every answer—even every emotion and thought of the 300 others—seems to be happening within me, yet it isn't disturbing. This epiphany grows in intensity and begins to feel extraordinarily blissful. The spaciousness that I've become is permeated with an all-pervading peace that connects us all; it is effortlessly holding anything discordant in a resonance of harmony.

I am aware that I can be as vast as I want to be, and can choose to expand anywhere and still be firmly planted in the room. At the same time, there is no *me* to find or even point to. Jenai has disappeared, and I am everything all at once. The experience of being in unity with everyone and everything in the room and beyond feels profound.

The fleeting thought that I may never find myself again or be able to function in the world in this state of bliss enters my mind. A feeling of peace encompasses my being, immediately showing me the absurdity of that thought. As my consciousness merges with something greater than a separate self, I realize that it's impossible to be separate from another.

Although I can't locate myself, I know that I was home—a place that was more my true self than any idea my mind had told me about myself leading up to that moment. I recognize myself as a soul connected to the wholeness of the Divine, as well as an intricate part of the human form that I chose to inhabit.

Something forever changed in me during the 90 minutes that I remained in this expansive state. My divinity and humanity had married and were now merged into one. The image of myself that I had projected to the world had completely dissolved into an experience of just being. Although I had conceptually understood the possibility of this for a long time—that I was a spirit having a human experience—this was the lived, felt sense of that truth.

Jenai Lane

I FEEL YOU

Settling in for a bus trip to New York City on a snowy winter day, the cold gray was also a feeling in my soul. Tired, sad, confused, and missing my daughter Cassandra, I boarded a bus from Massachusetts to spend the weekend with her. I was bringing Cassie her Christmas gift from her younger brother Skyler. I had just received it and was eager to see what it was and watch Cassie as she opened her gift.

In November, my talented and precious 17-year-old son, Skyler, was killed in a vehicular homicide. The kid who could make it through anything didn't make it through this accident. Sky was so young, smart, and strong. I would marvel at him jumping over the pool fence, pumping out hundreds of crunches at a time, and doing circus tricks on his unicycle like spin the diablo.

My world crashed down in a split second. How could something that lasted less than a minute, as the state police reported, affect your whole life and every minute within it? Death is like that.

Wanting to find a temporary sense of comfort from my grief, I put on my headphones and a guided meditation for the long ride, looking for the familiar buzzing feeling that had started to come to me. It felt like a bumble bee was stuck in my hair, like a tiny spot on my head was buzzing. It became my friend and I looked for it each day as something spiritual that also felt physical. The feeling was real. At times, I would pat my head and wipe back my hair just to make sure there wasn't a bug there, but there never was.

As I progressed in my practice, I'd talk to my supports and receive feedback to questions I had: *Why did the accident happen? Where did Skyler go? Is everything okay?* I would say in my moments of silence, *I'm sorry and I love and miss you, my son* . . . but I couldn't feel him.

As I continued to meditate consistently, I began to envision all that is in my heart and soul. The detailed pictures in my mind didn't always represent the real-life version, and this fascinated me. I would imagine my team of angels holding me up when I needed extra strength or walking a tight rope over the Grand Canyon when I felt stressed. I'd picture my worries safely tucked away in my purple velvet chest I named Hope, where they'd wait until I could give them the attention they needed.

Looking within, the little voice of Love would pop up right away and if I listened, I began to get answers to my questions.

Seven years later, it continues to grow and strengthen. I feel Spirit. I can feel my Skyler now. When I visualize my beautiful Angel Sky, his tingly invisible presence starts above my head, then passes over my lower legs, arms, and head.

Between meditating and reading every spiritual book I could get my hands on, I now know that Skyler is in a magical place, and that there is life after life, even though it's invisible to the human eye. Though gone from this earthly world, Skyler is still my son and always will be . . . so no matter where he is, I am his Mom. Yes, I am the mother of an angel, and am learning to live my life as one. My heart and soul still break but I am grateful for this blessing.

Seana A. Coughlin

THE GOLDEN TEMPLE

Each step of my trip to the sacred land of India felt Divinely orchestrated as my dear friend and I set out on a pilgrimage to the Shri Kashi Vishwanath Mandir, the Golden Temple of Lord Shiva in Varanasi. The city is known as the place of Shiva Lingams, one of the most worshipped representations of the Divine Feminine and Divine Masculine in all of India.

Upon our arrival at the Sathya Sai Maa Moksha Dham Ashram, where we were staying, which is located two blocks from the banks of the river Ganges, we were met with flower garlands from the loving devotees. It was a special evening as we would be taking part in an Arti Ceremony, a ceremony of light at the Kashi Vishwanth Temple.

Unfortunately, we arrived late to the temple due to traffic, showing our passports, packing our belongings into a locker, and filling out forms. The crowd was larger than expected so our host, Paresh, couldn't get us into the inner sanctum of the temple where the holy lingam is located and where the ceremony would be happening. The police guard instructed us to sit on the cement floor with several hundred others and watch the ceremony on a live feed television screen. We were disappointed that we couldn't be inside and physically part of the ceremony.

After a short while, I considered leaving because I felt disconnected from what was happening inside the heart of the temple. Paresh assured us, though, that he would do his best to get us in after the ceremony to touch the holy lingam.

We watched on the live feed as seven priests poured water, ghee, and milk over the lingam, which sat in a pure, golden square adorned with flowers. They offered light in the form of several arti lamps while powerfully chanting mantras that grew increasingly louder. Intense drumming was coming from the center of the temple, which drowned out all sound on the television. I could feel the energy vibrating in my heart and body.

When the ceremony ended, Paresh instructed us to quickly get up and follow him. The guard opened the gate just enough so we could slip inside. Paresh ushered us through a lot of commotion to the doorway of the inner sanctum. Suddenly, he motioned for me to go inside. Surrounded by men all speaking rapid-fire Hindi, I noticed that one man directly in front of the lingam had reached down and touched it with both of his hands.

As I got close to the lingam, I did the same . . . bending down to touch it with my right fingertips. The second I did so, a window between worlds opened up. A deep stillness and intense shakti entered my hand, went up my arm, and seemed to fill my every cell. I was transported to another time, another place, another life or lifetimes. Images and feelings passed through me, and a powerful feeling entered my eyes, my body, my mind, and touched my soul.

I fell into a black hole of complete stillness and profound power. Beneath my touch, the lingam felt hard, smooth, and soft all at the same time. This Divine stillness felt like it was from another dimension.

Someone bumped into me, and I became aware that I was being urged to move along, so I released my fingers from the lingam.

As I shuffled out of the crowded ashram and saw the long line of people waiting to get their few seconds with the holy lingam, I felt altered. I couldn't explain it to myself, let alone my companions. I didn't want to touch my hand to anything so that I could somehow keep the beyond-this-world connection with these sacred moments.

For the next few hours, I felt a need to stay quiet and just be with what had happened. As we rode back through the busy and bumpy streets of Varanasi in a three-wheeled tuk-tuk, I remained completely still inside as it all passed by.

Puja Sue Flamm

THE GODDESS KALI

*U*pon waking that morning, I felt a sense of heaviness and hopelessness.

This should be the most exciting time of my life, I thought.

My yoga studio was finally up and running, and the dullness of the corporate world was behind me. Something that I'd long desired had become reality, but on that sunny morning, excitement was missing.

My mind was preoccupied with something that had happened two weeks prior, when my husband of 15 years came home and announced that he was moving out. The moment I heard those words, layers of unsettling emotions flooded my body. I slumped into the chair and couldn't move. Weeks later, I was still feeling numb. Frozen. Stuck in something that no longer existed . . . an outdated version of me that I was desperately holding onto.

Lying in bed and watching a blue-faced honeyeater joyfully sucking nectar from a big tropical plant outside my window, I felt nothing but emptiness. Deep down I knew that this was it . . . this was the moment to let go of everything familiar and start anew, yet the thought of the world I knew so well crumbling down made me feel crushed and powerless. Could I move forward on my own? Knowing that there was no way back to my old life, or back to the old me, the unknown road ahead looked long, empty, and scary. There were no signs telling me which way to turn, which exit to take, when to slow down, and when it's okay to go full speed ahead.

Finally, I got out of the bed with the thought, *I should meditate to get centered and gain some clarity,* so I settled into a comfy chair and began.

With the smell of Frankincense wafting through the room and a gentle Mona Lisa smile on my face, my whole being began to relax into a state of bliss. I welcomed this sudden shift in my energy field and gave into it. The vibration of a kundalini force coursing through my body caused it to subtly sway.

Suddenly, a strange-looking female with a black face and a red tongue sticking out appeared in my inner vision. When I saw this face, I knew it resided somewhere deep in the core of my being. As my meditation continued, this female energy slowly started to emerge from the depths, growing bigger and bigger, until it came out of my body and stared right at my face.

I knew very little about the Goddess Kali, only her name and what her energy represented, but I had no idea what she looked like . . . until now. The moment my eyes met Kali's, I felt as though I was floating in an infinite space. All connection to physical reality disappeared; I completely lost any sense of the room I was in, along with the uncertainty, the numbness. Everything was gone.

Suddenly, I was surrounded by profound spaciousness where nothing else existed. The space was dark but not heavy, and there was something comforting, even nurturing, about it. Waves of warmth and renewed hope flooded my whole being. I knew that I was in the presence of a great teacher who was desperate to yank her student out of a slumber, so she doesn't waste another second in an illusion about herself and the potential she holds.

It was clear that Goddess Kali wanted me to get real. She wanted me to embrace the long road ahead with courage and faith. She wanted me to pay attention to the magical landscape on the side of that road and soak in every ounce of its beauty—the scent of the flowers, chirping of the birds, warmth of the sun on my skin. She wanted me to take this opportunity of a new beginning, and to embrace the rebirth with great wisdom and strength.

Goddess Kali arrived to wake up the warrior in me, to give me the power to make a leap into the unknown, to break out of the conventional notion of how life should be. Glancing at her once more before closing my meditation, her sword-like eyes cut through the chains of my old, limited self, invoking liberation and empowerment.

Slowly, I felt myself re-emerging from this womb of rebirth. Kali's face was gone and my awareness returned to physical reality, but a spark was ignited in my very core. At a chaotic time in my life when I was struggling to discern how to move forward, this was the priceless gift that Kali left.

Irina Morrison

THE SPACE TO CONNECT

*M*y son has a plastic toy in the shape of an interconnected sphere. It can be compressed into a small, tight sphere that looks almost solid but when pulled outward, the toy becomes both larger and less dense. I think we are like that sphere when we meditate—we create more space in the mind and body.

When I first began meditating, I sometimes felt like I was leaving my body. As I started to sense an expansion, feeling frightened I would immediately bring myself back into my physical body.

One day, I shared this with one of my friends who is an experienced meditator.

"What about it was scary?" she inquired.

"I felt like I was floating and . . . well . . . I was afraid to leave the space I know."

Just speaking this to her made it not seem so scary anymore. In fact, I wondered if this "fear of expansion" was metaphorically relevant to other parts of my life.

"You don't leave your body." she explained. "You just expand beyond your physical body. There is no space we know . . . there is only space."

Today, as I enter meditation, I don't have those fears. I close my eyes and let the thoughts ride because I know that if I try to stop them, they'll just come at me harder. I breathe. As my breath slows, my thoughts follow suit and my closed eyes begin to see. In my mind's eye, I see inner worlds and colors—purple at the point right between my eyebrows, my third eye. It starts as a small circle of light, gradually gets bigger, then fades and a new small circle starts to expand. As time passes unmeasured, the purple light's cycle of movement slows, then stops. Like virtual reality goggles, the color is in front of both my third eye and my two earthly eyes. It expands to my temples and I feel like I have bug eyes.

The light and color extend to the sides of my head. Every cell in my cranium is swimming in the created space. The sphere has opened. My inner energy field starts to radiate like the sun; and my aura, like a magic shield or "light body", surrounds me in warmth. It's not that I leave my body, but that my spirit body grows beyond my physical body—just like my friend explained.

My cells dance in the space around me. Less aware of my physical self, I travel beyond my thoughts and physical sensations.

Then, I sense into the universe. I connect without effort to everything in this world, the cosmos, and beyond. I see all time, or the timelessness of infinity. In these moments, I know it is a wisdom we all possess but rarely access. It lies deep within.

I'll show you, the Universe seems to say, *and then you cannot question it.*

With eyes still closed, I begin to see millions of little white triangles, outlined in red-green-blue, with a connecting line from the deepest recesses of my brain to the corner of my left eye. It reminds me of the inside of a television with millions of pixels and particles vibrating. I open my eyes and the triangles remain. More colors now . . . pink, orange, green . . . microscopic pixels connecting from my left eye to . . . well, everything.

I open my eyes and look towards the plant and candle on my table. My vision connects a thick line of triangles from my eye to them. Clear across the room, my son is sitting at the table, surrounded by even smaller particles but no less faint. I am reminded of an invisible cobweb that holds us all together—and that, for me now, is visible.

The message is in the feeling I'm getting—not scared of leaving my body or losing my vision or having a stroke. I can sense the Divinity of all things. Deep peace, calm, and joy. A feeling of fearlessness and bliss just in being; a dance on earth with the beautiful cosmos.

I am being given a sneak-peek opportunity to see beyond the veil of our everyday experiences—a tear in whatever invisible forces hold the universe together has opened a gateway into a visible, visual continuum.

As I look around with fascination and faith, I trace the line of vision to the plants, my table, the candle, my son—all grand connections in the field of energy. We are all occupying space together. We are one giant mass of particles and the concept of separation is the illusion.

I am the plant, and the plant is me. This Divine truth is being presented to me. The universe confirms my questions, my spiritual work, the mystery and magic—it all fades into a profound net that catches us all. Whatever our beliefs, we are all part of the same fabric of space. It makes complete sense.

Those moments of expansion felt eternal and brought me to another space beyond time. The meditation ended and I was back to earth—back with a message: to not fear, but be joyous because we are not alone. We are connected all to each other, creating our experiences together . . . and the access to this truth is so simple. To travel to the cosmos and see the Divine, just sit comfortably and close your eyes.

Jennifer Herrera

LOVE LOST AND FOUND AGAIN

*L*ife has a way of showing the path we are to walk. In the past, I resisted or didn't pay attention to signs from Spirit . . . until I had a meditation experience that took me between worlds.

Sinking slowly into this meditation, I began to have flashbacks of myself in different timelines in Egypt, the Civil War, Europe, and many other places. In some, I was male; in others, I was female. They zigzagged through my consciousness rapidly and with extraordinarily strong energy, feelings, and emotions.

Struggling to comprehend what was happening and what it all meant, the meditation progressed into an experience that brought me to my knees. The energy of the daughter I lost in pregnancy came through, as if I was holding her in my arms. Tears cascaded down my cheeks, and a tidal wave of emotions and memories erupted of this loss from 25 years earlier. It was more than I could handle. The reconnection to the experience of her death was the end of my life as I knew it and a new beginning into the world of Spirit.

Meditation had now become a part of my daily routine. I found solace in the inner world that presented answers and a peaceful connection to a deep part of who I am. Through the interweaving of the present and the past, I began to connect the dots. My understanding of why things were happening in my life began to make sense as I practiced and journaled my meditation experiences. It became a respite from the harsh realities, allowing me to settle into a space that is hard to reach when my mind is busy.

Deep breathing coupled with setting intention before going into meditation helps me to not get in my own way. Training in awareness has given me better perspectives, and the ability to observe my thoughts without judgment of the deep-rooted emotions. I can be present and not so attached to the past, taking the lessons from so much loss. Determined that those lessons would be about courage, strength, and perseverance in the face of adversity—with the endurance to take one step at a time, practicing forgiveness and acceptance—I was able to release the grip of what I had experienced so I could focus more on the joys of today.

It seems all that I had been through from birth to this juncture was entangled with lost love. In the past, I had love with my twin flame and soul mate . . . then he was gone. Eventually, we found each other again.

The heart wrenching pain of that loss—and its opening to the experience of the distant past and another lifetime—was even more crushing than what I felt with my daughter. His death left a hole in my heart bigger than the oceans of the world, and it took me a long time to move past the emotions of betrayal, hurt, anger, and revenge for the person who took his life.

As destiny would have it, slowly but surely, in meditation our lives came together again . . . I should say, slammed together! Without the intention to find this lost love, the web of connectivity coursed through each of our lives to reunite us.

Love found its way back to me through meditation, visions, and an inner compass guiding me along the way. I found a pathway into my being once again to heal, hope, and reunite with what had been so abruptly taken away.

Eileen Bild

TRANSCENDENCE

One Sunday, my mom, brothers, and I returned home from church and found my father sitting in the living room in his patterned boxers with his eyes closed and legs crossed in a lotus position.

In one hand, he held a carrot; in the other, a tomato. With sunlight streaming golden rays across his face, he resembled an ad in a yoga magazine. Utterly intrigued, I stared in fascination.

"Dad, what are you doing?" I asked, breaking the silence.

"Shhhh . . . I'm trying to reach *samadhi*."

Unaffected by my intrusion, he continued to sit in perfect silence as I stood, wide-eyed and motionless, completely enthralled.

Having just returned from hearing a Sunday sermon, my father's comment sparked a surprise lesson into the roots of religion. As I would later learn, ancient yogis perfect this same state of *samadhi* that my dad was trying to attain. Observing him that day, my mind conjured images of faraway lands and epic battles over Truth. Echoes of good versus evil . . . right versus wrong . . . light versus dark . . . rang through my mind and shone before me like a polestar, beckoning me to follow it.

In those moments, and at that tender age of five years old, I pledged allegiance to something far greater than myself—a force beyond my understanding that would always keep me heading in the right direction and striving for something higher. It was a path in search of God and, somehow, I knew even then that I was in for a life of intrigue.

All these years later, as I look back on my spiritual journey, I clearly remember the day that my spiritual path took a marked turn upward. I was 23 years old and in a room with my teacher, surrounded by candles, incense, fruit, and flowers. Sitting quietly with my eyes closed while he performed a sacred ceremony, I began to sink into my subconscious like a falling, drifting leaf. I went beyond the subconscious into a place of pure silence.

Suddenly but naturally, my mind opened into sheer unbounded awareness; nothingness yet everything-ness at the same time. In my heart, in my life, in my journey, the clouds literally parted, and I became immersed in the pure light of God. There was no sense of anything but this. No thought, only awareness... only God and only light... pure, unbounded consciousness ... stillness ... and the fulfillment of that Sunday-after-church experience that my dad was trying to achieve. Jesus taught that the Kingdom of Heaven is within. Heaven's doors quietly opened wide that day ... and my heart fell to its knees.

That day I found the whole me, the real me, in that profound experience of silence that surpasses all understanding—and, of course, the first person with whom I shared the experience was my father.

Margo Lenmark

CHRISTMAS AT THE OASIS

ordering on physical and emotional burnout, I decide to take a respite at my favorite desert spa known for its healing water. These restful few days at the oasis consisted of soaking in the hot mineral springs, receiving massages, spending a lot of time in silence reading spiritual books, sleeping in a little cabin, and meditating.

Typically opting for a mantra meditation, one morning I turned on a guided recording and within seconds of closing my eyes, a vision appeared of a very large rabbit sitting near my feet. As soon as I noticed him, he hopped away through a beautiful, lush forest. I followed, which caused him to hop faster and faster. Soon I was running to keep up with him. Suddenly I took off and began flying through the air, all the way to the edge of the forest. The rabbit vanished, but I kept flying.

In front of me was a snow-covered mountain with a stream running down and a little wooden platform nearby. Landing on the platform, I found myself face to face with a monk in a deep burgundy robe. He had a gentle, compassionate countenance.

Thank you for taking time to visit me, he said, then after a while, he added, *It is time to continue your journey.*

Once again, I was flying through the air towards another mountain, this one green and tropical with craggy peaks. I noticed a small golden temple next to a waterfall, so I landed at the door and went in.

Although it was quite dark inside, a skylight illuminated a giant orchid in the middle of the room. While trying to get my bearings, an older woman, much older than me, with long gray hair, emerged from the orchid and walked toward me. A little girl peaked out from behind her skirt. I had a knowing that this girl was me at the age of three. She was wearing a black-and-white, polka-dot party dress and pink Mary Jane shoes.

The old woman and the child seemed overjoyed to see me. They both hugged me and thanked me for coming, and I soaked up their love.

We commend you for taking the time out of your busy life to rest and renew yourself, the woman commented. *Now it's time to go.*

She showed me to the door at the back of the temple. *When you're ready, open the door and step through it.*

Still quite dark, I closed my eyes and took a giant step forward. When my foot landed on solid ground, I opened my eyes.

Surprisingly, I found myself standing inside the middle of a huge Christmas tree. Twinkling lights encircled me, and the tree was decorated with ornaments that I instantly remembered seeing on other families' trees as a child. Being raised Jewish, my family never had a yuletide tree. In fact, I questioned whether either Santa Claus or Jesus had ever really existed.

Yet, there he was, directly in front of me . . . Old Saint Nick, sitting in a sizable ornate chair. He motioned for me to come and sit on his lap. I walked over, sat down, and put my arm around his neck. Staring at his face, I recognized his eyes and eyebrows and realized that I was looking into my own eyes.

What do you want for Christmas? Santa Claus asked. I immediately began to recite a long list of things that I'd always wanted. *You shall have them all.*

In that instant, a large cross of light streamed down from the top of the tree. I reached my arm up behind Santa and put it around the cross. The cross slowly lifted me up, up, up . . . through the top of the tree and into the night sky.

I was flying again, this time with the cross. Suddenly, the cross of light transformed into Jesus. For the next few minutes, I laid in Jesus' arms, transfixed, as he flew me across the night sky.

It's true . . . you really do exist! I said in awe, looking into his compassionate eyes. *You're real. You're really real.*

Jesus simply smiled and gazed at me with an expression that can only be described as pure unconditional love.

A moment later, I was sitting in my chair in the little cabin at the oasis.

Arielle Ford

VISIONING THE GRAND PALACE

*G*rowing up in the 1960s, the life and work of Rev. Dr. Martin Luther King, Jr. deeply impacted my sense of the possible, especially in terms of sacred service. At the same time, girls of my generation faced a daunting challenge. The culture of that era dictated that leadership was beyond a woman's grasp.

In spite of this, as a young girl, I was gifted with visions from the Divine that I would one day become both a doctor and a minister.

"Women can't be doctors, or ministers, or CEOs, or rabbis," my mother informed me.

Acceptable career choices were being a nurse or an actress, so I chose the creative path. As I ventured into the performing arts world, it became my spiritual path, and I sensed a Divine plan at play. The more courageously I surrendered to my authentic gifts, the visions that I'd had as a child became clearer and the Divine messages became louder.

As my life progressed and I developed a meditation practice, I began to honor my visions more courageously and respect my spiritual intuition. One recurring vision in my meditations was of a remarkably large theater, with rows and rows of plush, red velvet seats surrounded by intricate, golden worlds of wonder. This theater called to me as if it existed somewhere in the physical world. I trusted that my heart's longing for this magnificent place would someday be fulfilled. So, as I visited and performed at venues around the world, I searched for this grand theater.

As I grew more mature, the world around me changed. I returned to school, studied theology and spiritual practice, and was ordained as an interfaith minister. One of my childhood visions had been realized.

In 2015, I was asked if I would be interested in becoming the Chief Executive Officer and Spiritual Director of the United Palace, located on Broadway in Manhattan. Spanning an entire city block, it is among the most ornate landmark theatres in New York with rows of plush, red velvet seats, all of which are surrounded by intricate and exquisite golden art.

Recently, I've been working on my doctorate—another childhood Divine vision soon to be realized. I am a reverend leading a spiritual community based at the United Palace that is grounded in an idea called Spiritual Artistry. We celebrate Divine Spirit in all its manifestations, including the arts, culture, and entertainment.

In everything I do now, I remember to honor the visions and believe the dreams, as they are, in fact, letters from Divine dimensions.

Bishop Heather Shea

CAN YOU HEAR ME NOW?

*G*od, the Sacred, has quite a sense of humor.

Truthfully, I never wanted to be a church pastor. Having grown up knowing about God and having a deep faith, several people, seemingly out of the blue, would drop hints that I should follow the path of ministry.

This was the last thing on my mind as I was driving one bright, beautiful day to present a workshop at a women's retreat sponsored by the church I was attending. My thoughts on the drive were more consumed with practical matters, as I was in the process of selling one home and making an offer on another that I really wanted. Assuming that the weekend workshop would be a fertile place to set intentions, I planned to ask God for direction about my life and specifically about this new home. I had no idea that there was something much more important on God's mind.

Upon arrival at the retreat, I greeted everyone with love, joy, and laughter, and settled in for the weekend feeling free, light, and full of excitement. Attendees were already engaged in deep conversations, and the music playing in the center was praiseful and moving. During the liturgical dancing and the words spoken during that first evening of the retreat, I felt God's presence.

Everyone was filled with the Spirit and in awe of all that God was doing in our lives.

When I joined the plenary session the next morning, one of my favorite preachers and mentors was giving a sermon. I made a mental note to ask her about an important issue that was brewing in our denomination, then settled into a contemplative state—pen and notebook in hand—ready to absorb and notate her inspirational words.

The reverend began to recount her call to ministry, sharing her belief that she would do ministry later in her life, but that God had a different plan.

"Can you hear me now?" she recalled God saying to her after making other plans to become an adolescent clinical therapist.

Ouch! Ouch! Whoa! Is she speaking directly to me?

I couldn't believe the similarities in our calling. For years, I too, had chosen to work as a psychologist, a career that had taken me years and years and years of schooling. What I enjoyed about it was helping and serving others. Despite knowing internally that there was more for me to do, I refused to accept the nudge deep within that I was being called to a ministry of pastoring.

For the rest of this reverend's sermon in that morning session, as I sunk deeper into contemplation, every word pierced my soul, as though they were meant just for me.

How did she know about my conversation with God? I had not told anyone!

By the end of the sermon, I was an emotional wreck—stomach churning, stunned, and in a state of shock. In this contemplative state, I knew beyond a shadow of a doubt that God was speaking directly to me through my mentor.

Can you hear me now, Terrlyn? God seemed to say. I have been calling you, but for some reason you don't seem to understand or want to admit it.

This was the moment when I stopped running, and my encounter with God that day stayed with me. I drove home from the retreat feeling humbled, filled with curiosity, and truthfully, a little afraid, pondering the ways my life would change.

Yet through those contemplative moments at the retreat, I finally felt assured that I was being called into the sacred work of pastoring, shepherding, and guiding folks in a religious setting, and to model and teach the importance of manifesting the God within us and seeing the Divine in everyone . . . knowing that God would walk with me every step of the way. *Yes, God. I can hear you now!*

Rev. Dr. Terrlyn L. Curry Avery

METAMORPHOSIS

eing raised by a Roman Catholic mother and a Hindu father, I often wondered as a child, *Is there one God or 33 million gods?* My parents each had different ways of worshipping the Divine, and through observing them, I came to understand my Creator as an interpretation . . . at least until I'd one day figure out what this all meant for me personally.

Growing up, I was petrified of priests, gurus, and anything religious. I couldn't set foot in a church or be in front of a guru. In fact, if I found myself walking by a neighborhood place of worship, I would literally cross the street in order to keep as far away from it as possible.

We had a picture of the Brahma Kumaris founder, Brahma Baba, in my childhood home, and his eyes had a way of following me everywhere I went in the house. It was quite annoying, especially during my teenage years, when all I wanted to do was go out and live life my own way. On many occasions, Baba's eyes would emerge in my consciousness, as if watching out for my safety and wellbeing. Not to say that I didn't get myself in trouble, but even when I did, the vision of his eyes would exude compassion and guidance, protecting me from getting into anything that wouldn't have been healthy for me.

Because of my parents' connection to the Brahma Kumaris, I was surrounded by some of the most powerful woman yogis in history. To me, they were just my friends that I got to hang around with. I didn't have the inclination to focus on my spiritual life, as they did, and as my parents subtly encouraged me to do.

"Jen, never forget that the world behind your eyes is the real world," my mom and dad would always tell me. "Your body is the vehicle, but you, the soul, are the driver. Always remember that you have the power to drive and go wherever you want to go."

That thought stayed with me . . . and they would also tell me about the energy of God's light, and how it is connected to the best part of you, the part that dreams of having the fullest existence possible.

By the age of 20, I was living my own dream life—at least, what I thought at the time was the ultimate road to happiness and success. It was about as far removed from a yogic lifestyle as anyone can get. I owned and managed two nightclubs in Miami—one in South Beach and another in Key Biscayne. It was a time in my life when I got to throw all of my creativity and female dynamism into these business ventures.

Outwardly, I was the queen dame around town—Jenny from the block—running my clubs, dressed to the nines in designer clothes, and cruising around in either my BMW, Jaguar, or Mercedes Benz. My daily routine was party, sleep, repeat: get to the clubs by 10 o'clock, dance and socialize all night, and make it home just as the sun was rising over the ocean. Home was a luxury condominium with a large central living area, where I strategically positioned a black-and-red, Italian-made sofa towards the window, overlooking the beautiful Atlantic shoreline.

Sitting on that couch one day, for whatever reason, I began to ponder some of these ideas that my parents and yogi friends had instilled in me about the power of God's light. I became curious: *I wonder what it is they are feeling.*

As I'm in this state of contemplation, watching the waves crash one after another after another on the beach, suddenly my five senses, as well as my face and hands, began to morph into nothing but light energy. This light slowly engulfed me until I was no longer there. All of my being was subtly vacuumed into the energy of Light, of the soul, of the driver who was governing the vehicle. Even the vehicle disappeared, and the only thing remaining was the driver. It felt like the soul was attaching the energy of itself to my five human senses in order to give it identity.

Oh, my God, I've completely lost it, I thought. My reaction was one of fear. *I've got to come back . . . I've got to come back.*

Panic overtook me, as I didn't want to let go of anything that I'd become attached to in my life—not just the success, the friends, the accoutrements, the popularity, the ambition, but also simply being a woman in a human body.

Having no idea how long this sensation went on—between one second and five hours—I eventually got up from the couch and walked to the bathroom. Being able to lift my body and move across the room was the only way I could recognize that I was still in physical form.

Gazing into the bathroom mirror, I could see only half of my face. The other half was in the form of my consciousness, like a hologram of my existence that I could splice my hand through. I could vaguely see a skeletal structure, but the overall visage was sublime, like I was metamorphosing right before my eyes.

Feeling completely freaked out by this sensation, I tried for some time to force my consciousness back into matter. Finally, I was able to shake myself fully back into self-awareness and was able to see my entire body in front of me in the mirror. Once I did, I felt back in control yet, ironically, noticed that I immediately missed that sensation of being so free and unincumbered by form.

Composing myself enough to grab my phone, I called my mom and explained to her as best I could what had just happened.

"What *was* that?" I asked.

"It's okay. You've had a subconscious experience that is preparing you to receive God's light."

"God's light?"

"Yes, dear. Did you feel peace? Did you feel love?"

"Uh, no. I didn't feel *any* of that. It was scary."

"It's okay. That's why the more you study and understand these mystical truths, the more you become a master of them."

That mystical experience set me on a quest to discover how to bring that liberated, true, sentient vibe of the soul into my life. Soon, I found myself wanting this vibration in everything I did: making business deals, having relationships, cooking, cleaning, traveling, and just sitting. I began to release the fear of religion that I'd been carrying, and followed my curiosity to explore the beauty of the spiritual. From then on, my whole life changed. How I saw the world, through the love of this Divine light, had changed.

My eventual journey with the Brahma Kumaris offered me the scaffolding upon which to experiment with bringing that Divine awareness and energy into my five senses. Have I mastered it? No, not yet, but I am well on my way.

Sister Dr. Jenna

PART THREE

Deepening Your Connection to the Divine through Meditation

What a man takes in by contemplation, that he pours out in love.

—MEISTER ECKHART

THE WORLD BEHIND YOUR EYES

———————•◦●◦•———————

*P*ositioned in front of our booth at an exhibition that my organization sponsored in Washington, D.C., was a large banner that posed a simple yet profound question: Who am I?

During the first day of the exhibition, a particular attendee breezed past our booth, then stopped in her tracks as she caught sight of the banner.

"I know who *I* am," she said with an attitude. "Do *you*?"

Slightly perplexed, our entire crew quietly pondered how to respond to her remark from their private, interior worlds. As the woman walked away, they noticed her flamboyant style of dress, carefully coiffed hair, and perfectly drawn makeup, and could have made a quick judgment. They found themselves curious to explore why she had made this remark, and if there was something they could learn from it for themselves.

The next day, the woman returned to our booth after attending my presentation that morning about the importance of meditation.

"Hearing you speak and feeling your energy, I realized that you definitely know yourself," she shared with me, as I observed that her countenance had softened. "Maybe I *don't* know myself. I want to explore this further. Can you help me?"

Meditation has various ways of being interpreted. A simple exploration of an encounter like the one with this woman at the exhibition can be coined as a meditation moment, an opportunity to discover more of yourself. So, when someone tells me they can't meditate, I tend to not believe them. As I mentioned earlier, everybody has quiet moments in the shower or at night before drifting off to sleep.

How does one expand these contemplative moments into a deeper experience? This is a journey of acclimating thoughts, words, and actions from a deeply awakened state of being. By "awakened", I mean to see more than what your two eyes see. It means to interpret the moment from a place where silence meets wisdom, and to value the purpose of your existence.

I would say to you, as I did to the conference goers that day, to consider the world behind your eyes—the inner space where the experience occurs. Understand that you are an immortal, eternal, imperishable being of light, a soul that's been on a long journey. Now place your consciousness on that inner pull of the eternal, which is like an ocean of peace, truth, and power. See if you have the openness and the patience to just allow the energy of that connection to somehow influence you for a little bit. Invite it in and allow it to pour into you . . . gently, subtly, deeply.

OVERCOMING BLOCKS TO THE PROCESS

Mental blocks to this fluid, love-filled process arise from having an expectation or certain interpretation of meditation. If your mind is scattered when you sit down to meditate, this could be a sign that you're not paying attention to yourself. If when you want to have a quiet moment with yourself, and find that you can't be still or comfortable, this is your cue that you're not taking care of yourself. Step back and tend to what you need based on what your intuition is telling you.

Another thing I notice with many well-intentioned meditators is that there is a limitation in how they are perceiving what they're going through in their lives. For example, people who are in a particular situation, whether it's their marriage or their career or a health issue, tend to focus their energy only on what's not working. It turns into a vicious cycle and then, unbeknownst to them, they become stuck in this web for a month, a year, 10 years, 30 years.

If you can relate to this, I encourage you to try your best to not pull your energy from other people or things that might make you believe those interpretations. Turn ever inward when seeking your answers, and embrace the process of self-discovery. Just being in self-inquiry, nothing more, can be exuberant and edifying.

In overcoming blocks to a full meditation experience, it is important to understand that truly mystical experiences do not come through the ego-mind. The ego can never explain what a Divine experience is like. It's not supposed to, because it doesn't speak the language. Mystical moments are often so profound, in fact, that they mostly defy words. For this reason, don't fall into the mind trap of overanalyzing or trying to define your mystical moments, especially to others. Keep them unto yourself, with no words necessary.

If you feel resistance to the process of meditation and can't seem to overcome it, please know that this, too, has its benefit. You see, oftentimes, the blockages are a way for us to not feel the hurt, pain, or trauma that may be a part of our soul's journey. It's like your soul intuitively knows that it's not yet time for you to move back into soul awareness. It knows that you're not quite ready to see how beautiful and powerful you are, or to comprehend the ways in which God's beauty can work through you.

When you reach a point where you say, "Okay, I don't think I want to keep feeling this pain or acting out in anger, insecurity, or fear just because I'm bruised inside," this is when the blocks to meditation will begin to subside and release. When you are truly ready, after building the courage and strength, you will see that time was kind to you, and now your meditative journey can begin. You will ask the right internal questions, signaling to the soul that you are poised to finally be free of the bondage.

Little by little, it will bring you back into a comfortable space of introspection, and you will open so beautifully to your soul's remembrance of who you are. This is why mystical encounters come through being humble and surrendered to the soul's consciousness, which is an element of awareness in your personality based in self-respect. Don't be surprised if this process makes you quieter, kinder, and more contemplative, because now you are aware that you are carrying something so sacred.

HOW MEDITATION CHANGES YOU

Meditation allows us to come back to a place of inner balance, where our thoughts, feelings, energy, and time are used in a way that has value and is worthwhile. Everything depends on our stage of awareness and an understanding of our true identity. As we deepen into our practice, we start to open the door to more positive experiences in life. We begin to value things of a spiritual rather than a material nature. We desire to create a values-based life, where we can afford to be generous and loving. Our thinking becomes clearer and our decision-making power increases.

Embracing contemplation and meditation will reveal healthier, more joyful ways to live. For example, you may be inspired to change your diet to a more vegetarian-based one, or your lifestyle to one that is simpler and more focused on your virtues. You will eventually begin to understand that your life can be used for a higher purpose, which we will elaborate on in an upcoming chapter.

Creating a space for the Divine will enable profound insights to be revealed to you, as they have for the individuals whose stories you've just read. Feelings of belonging, seeing the Divinity in others, gentle urgings to follow your soul's path, and even feeling yourself *as* a soul are all ways that you will begin to feel a stronger sense of spiritual empowerment. You will begin to respond to situations, rather than reacting to them.

This creates harmony in all things, happier and healthier relationships, and can change your life in the most positive ways, because it encourages you to stay authentic and simple in a natural way that is not forced.

TYPES OF MEDITATION

So, how to begin? There are probably as many ways to meditate as there are souls on earth. The type of meditation that attracts you will depend on what you are looking for. Are you seeking a tool for stress reduction? Improved concentration? Getting to know yourself better? Or, simply connecting with the Divine?

Some commonly known practices offer a more structured approach that can give you a foundation for how and where to start. Here are a handful of the most widely used types of meditation, beginning with my personal favorite.

RAJA YOGA: This ancient form of meditation is practiced with the eyes open, which makes it versatile and easy to incorporate into your daily activities. Raja Yoga trains the mind to be your friend and gives you the inclination to choose loving, positive thoughts over those which are negative and wasteful. I like to say that Raja Yoga sets you free because it releases the power to respond with love.

We all make mistakes. We all waste our words, energy, and time until we pause and think deeply about what matters in our lives. When we hold on tightly to our views, the mind shrinks and smothers any power to love. In that state, the soul can't breathe new energy into a situation, and everyone loses. But when we sit quietly, canceling all mindsets, and allow ourselves to know the deep peace of the soul, miraculous changes can happen for the better. People will understand you more clearly, new doors will open, and you will feel more relaxed overall.

This is the power of Raja Yoga. It teaches you to step back and observe life, take a calm breath, cool your reactions, and go forward in a manner that is independent of others urging you to think or act as they wish.

GUIDED MEDITATION: Before awakening our consciousness to the broadest, highest perspective, we may see the world around us from a very average point of view. These thoughts are connected to a more limited sense of purpose. I'm not saying that purpose is not important, but our thoughts that are joined to that interpretation and intent are typically based on a smaller sense of identity.

As we awaken and open to another version of ourselves, we sometimes need a little bit of guidance and support until we acclimate to this new way of being. Awakening means that we're willing to transform the way we see ourselves. This is where guided meditation can be very useful. It helps you to connect with what your awakening feels like for you. You can begin to have an intimate, ongoing conversation with yourself in your guided meditations.

There are many varieties of guided meditations to choose from by well-known meditation experts, and based on what your soul needs, you will resonate with a particular person's approach. At some point in time, when you are rooted comfortably in your awakened self, you may find that your guided meditations become just one sentence, and that will be all you need … until they become just one word, and that will be all you need.

Eventually, you won't even need one word. You will be in the embodiment of what has been created as a result of your process so far.

MANTRA MEDITATION: It is helpful, at times, to meditate on a mantra, which creates a calming in your personality when used consistently over a period of time. It is a tool to direct you to, ultimately, where the soul wants to go.

Mantra meditation can be practiced by selecting a word, phrase, or prayer that resonates with you on the deepest level. You should be able to repeat it easily and naturally, so that you don't have to think about it. Quietly repeat the mantra for a set of recitations, about 10 or 20, then begin to recite it silently. As thoughts arise, return to the mantra. This practice will help you experience the present moment more fully and, therefore, make more conscious choices.

WALKING MEDITATION: This form of meditation is perfect for individuals who don't necessarily feel comfortable sitting and contemplating the thoughts emerging in their minds. It can be done by mostly anyone, and doesn't require any special equipment or resources.

I recommend going for a walk in the morning hours, either in silence or accompanied by a guided meditation of your choosing. Doing this outdoors in nature is ideal, though it can be done in a large, quiet interior space, as well. As you begin, walk at a natural pace with your hands placed wherever comfortable.

To add a mantra-type experience, count your steps up to 10 or 20, then pause and begin again. With every step, be mindful of your body moving in cadence with your mantra or thoughts as they arise.

SOUND MEDITATION: Sound meditation connects us to vibrational frequencies that reside inside of the soul. It is an ancient practice that has been used by many cultures and wisdom traditions to restore a state of balance. You may find that music, chanting, toning, or immersing in a sound bath helps to shift you into a calmer, clearer perspective. It can incorporate the use of sacred instruments—such as the gong, didgeridoo, singing bowls, cymbals, and bells—to release energetic blockages and ease you into a more harmonic frequency.

Even if you have never meditated, you can experience less tension and anxiety after just a single sound healing session. The frequencies aren't just heard; they are felt through tactile physical vibrations. Today, the use of binaural beats is more widespread, as studies advance in how the human brain works. Binaural beats help brainwave frequencies to synchronize, leading you into a state of deep relaxation associated with beta waves, or creative flow associated with meditative theta waves. It's a beautiful, melodic practice.

CONTEMPLATIVE PRAYER: It's important for us to broaden our definition of contemplative prayer, especially if you are new to meditation. To me, it simply means that when you're having a thought, with alert awareness you pause at a particular point in the journey of that thought, and go into deeper introspection. The prayer aspect is simply the curiosity and questioning of, *What does that thought actually mean in terms of who I need to be or who I will become?* It is a practice of preparing yourself to ask the right questions for yourself in your future becoming.

Incorporating contemplative prayer into your life enables you to enjoy who you are becoming at every step of the way. It deepens your sense of self-trust, and you will come to understand yourself even more. You can ask the right questions, such as, *Can I trust the thoughts that I'm having? Can I trust the words I'm about to speak? Can I even trust my future?* Without contemplation, you are subject to everything that is happening in front of your eyes.

Mostly all of that is a manifestation of thoughts you've had in the past, or thoughts that others have had in the past. So, ask yourself, *Why would I want my soul to be influenced by an orange that's already been squeezed? Why am I still trying to get juice from it?*

MEDITATIVE READING: It is often helpful to take inspiration from sacred texts and authentic spiritual literature as part of your meditative practice. I enjoy reading timeless spiritual classics like the *Bhagavad Gita*, which I find to be very meditative. It is also useful to read about the experiences of others who have chosen to turn inward, such as the authors in this book.

In such stories and books, you can often find in one sentence something that can take you very deep inside and give you a realization about yourself. This phenomenon happens because enlightened masters throughout time have used meditation as an important tool for channeling their energy, as well as conserving their energy so that it had more impact. The intention coming through their words has had the power to be felt by the minds of millions, and thousands of years later, they are still having an impact.

When choosing meditative reading, it's important for you to intuitively feel if it's coming from an authenticated place. Can you feel the intention of the book when you hold it in your hands and gently turn the pages? Can you sense the life in it? It's also important to get an idea about the author's journey. Who is speaking? What is it about the person's journey that you feel deserves your time and energy to commit to dive into it?

All of these practices are a refueling of the energy that is needed to create new ideas with whatever is in front of you, or add onto it, or make more of it. With meditation, you're moving your attention away from feeding on something old, and toward living from something new that's been created inside of you.

It's quite fascinating, and it's why we're here—to be truly alive, and to feel something about this gift of Life.

A SIMPLE PRACTICE

———— ··•◉•·· ————

The great prophets and seers had a handle on the interior journey, and for good reason. It's essential for each of us to live the highest expression of our human existence. As we've evolved over time, many people have defined and created brands around certain types of contemplative practices, but meditation doesn't need to be owned by any particular entity, group, or movement.

While I encourage you to experiment with and find the type of meditation that works best for you, I would like to offer some practical guidelines to follow when establishing and deepening your practice.

Rise Early. Give value to having an early morning routine. I rise somewhere around dawn. For me, the hours between two and four o'clock are sacred. When I get up at this time, it's like everything in the world is connected to a deeper sound and I can really see inside of myself and what I need to address. Ask the Divine to reveal to you how you can be of greatest use in your day. Take the essence of this morning routine with you as you travel through your day, revisiting that place of internal stillness. This doesn't require closing your eyes, or being alone. As you learn how to create a quiet space within yourself, you'll find that you can slip into it at any time. When there are people around you, or when the world is noisy or challenging, step into the silent space of the soul.

Create a Sacred Space. Dedicate a specific space in your home or in your workplace where you call it your sacred space. Even if it's simply a corner nook with a comfortable chair, this is the space that you go into with the utmost of purest of intentions to come out a better version when you leave it. Thoughts carry vibrations, so bring into this space only your highest thoughts and intentions. Keep a regular promise to yourself to show up in this space at an appointed time of your own making.

Keep Note of Your Meditation Thoughts. One of the things that I feel is imperative in the contemplation and meditation journey is to always keep a notebook next to your bedside or close by. Here, you can reflect on your deepest thoughts, fears, joys, thrills, and desires. The physical process of writing somehow gives wind to what your next choice needs to be, first internally then externally.

Read Spiritual Teachings. As I mention in the previous chapter, I find it imperative to have spiritual teachings nearby, and to draw on their wisdom. Make this mandatory in your practice. Every morning, put into your consciousness a love letter from God to yourself. This sets the tone for your day in such a way that you won't get easily thrown off by what is happening in your outer world. What you decide to take into yourself in the form of spiritual teachings should be the choice of your individual soul. If the spiritual knowledge you're leaning into becomes dogmatic and judgmental—not necessarily the teaching but the interpretation of it—then continue searching until you find the right fit.

Nourish Your Temple. Pay attention to the food you put inside of your beautiful human frame, because it impacts the way you think and feel. I like to follow a vegetarian diet, but the choice is up to you and your particular constitution. Always be conscious of the foods you eat, how much you eat, and how fast you eat it. Limit alcohol and follow a plant-based diet of real, live food instead of processed items devoid of energy and nutrients.

Enter Sleep Peacefully. Before sleep is a good time for your final meditation of the day. Book yourself a little time, as part of your bedtime routine, to sit quietly with yourself and reflect on the day, considering what was done well and what could be done differently tomorrow. Deliberately close up the files of the day's activities and put them away in your mind, so you can bring the day to a close and allow yourself to slip into sleep, untroubled and at peace.

Retreat. As needed and when you can, unplug from your devices and get away from your routine to do something that feeds your soul, or to do nothing at all but recharge. Create a sanctuary. Drop the distractions. Turn off your phone. Listen to soothing music. Simply enjoy the solitude and some unstructured time. You can even use this time to review recent events, create new dreams, or retreat into your inner space to renovate the soul. Besides creating oases of calm and quiet throughout each day, or a little sanctuary to unwind and relax, you might decide to break from your normal routine altogether and go on a spiritual retreat. In this safe space, you can go deeper within the core of your being and reconnect with your true spiritual self, the part of you that does not change.

These are the things that I do on a regular basis, and one more I can leave you with is to see people as your teachers. Never disregard a single person who enters your life and think that they're not there to show you something about yourself. They are, and they will.

Be mindful of the company you keep, the images you absorb, and the respect that you give to others and all living things. Spend time in nature absorbing sunlight and fresh air. This timeless advice has been part of folklore for centuries, but in these modern times, many of us have abandoned this simple wisdom.

When you listen to the world behind your eyes, it will continue to signal you that you're here to serve, and that you don't have to wait for something to be given to you before you give, which is what we will discuss next.

THE PATH OF SEVA

ne of the many gifts of meditation is that the soul receives a vision of its capacity to develop into an instrument of selfless service, or *seva,* and therefore, peace. The proof of the power of your contemplative practices is when your life's purpose begins to evolve more into wanting to serve others. This impulse arises as a natural consequence of understanding the spiritual truths of Divine love.

Being of service to others takes the concept of meditation and elevates it even higher by integrating it into our earthly existence. You begin to see an ever more expansive vision of how to take the gifts that you receive in meditation, and pour them out into the world. Giving to others in this way is like an insurance for your future, because you ultimately become the beneficiary of your own generosity.

When I first came onto my path of awakening, I wasn't initially interested so much in rules, principles, and learning to harness spiritual energy. The big appeal for me was the ability to be of service and to help humanity become a little better than it has been in my generation.

About four years into my spiritual journey, I realized that being of any service at all required me to have a deep awareness of my own value as an individual. It would come from me showing up in a way that I wasn't serving from something unfulfilled from my past, but rather from the fulfillment of my current narrative, knowing that I am connecting to Source, and that the Divine is using me to be of service.

This revelation definitely added to my humility, which in turn broadened my capacity to reach farther and wider in terms of understanding humanity, including myself. It made me feel very quiet about the way the Divine is working in my life and in others' lives through me. I feel it as a subtle, pure, invisible, yet visible Presence.

You will begin to observe that when the Divine is moving in you, your attachments to the ego-self are no longer in your motives. When that I-me-mine energy is out of your personality and intent, there's space for the energy of God's light to flow through you.

Great service is given anytime you can touch the heart and mind of another. When you can do that, it is the Divine working through you. Being of real service is when you impact another by giving them the courage to look inside of themselves and see their diamond, their worth, their light . . . and you take whatever the Creator has said through you or done through you as *their* treasure for *their* journey, to open up something new for them, so *they* can shine and live more fully. In return, the person feels it so profoundly that they instinctually hold the service that is extended to them in sacred trust, with nobility and respect.

SEVA BEGINS WITH YOU

Early on when I first began to dedicate myself to meditation, I was eager to announce to the whole world how good this felt. *Everyone has to learn to meditate and everything will be great!* I thought. *The world is going to become heaven, and I'm going to be a big part of it because I'm going to teach people how to do this!*

As I say above, I came to realize after those first few years that it's not the world that has to change. *I* have to change. That is when I started to recognize that the first meaning of seva is to serve yourself by applying certain spiritual principles into your life. First, you must stand on your own feet and make life decisions from a place of personal empowerment, always leading with love.

It begins with noticing the little things and bringing awareness to everything you do—being conscious when you're walking and when you're speaking, remembering the Divine when you're going to bed and waking up. These small yet important details through which you serve yourself eventually play out in big ways.

Once you're in this realm of consciousness for some time, you begin to see that there's a greater capacity within you to give, to contribute, to be kind. Reflecting back to before the awakening that occurred in your meditations, you start to recognize that previously, you were taking more than you were giving. *I'm not going to give you love until I see it first from you. I don't have to give you money unless you have something to offer me.* It begins to dawn on you that those with a taker mentality get tired easily and wear out, whereas those who are bestowing to others become energized and inspired. They ask, *Have I given more than I've taken? How much more can I give? How much more can I serve?*

These questions find their answers when you begin to contemplate your own unique skills and talents when balanced with spiritual integrity. You become intrigued with how the energy of Source can use you to bring light into the world, whether it's in your home, community, company, or other relationships. This means that the tasks you are required to complete— whether mopping a floor or chairing an important meeting—take on a different fragrance and attitude than if you were doing these things out of anger or an expectation of getting something you want. Seva means *I'm not going to wait for you to give me something before I show up being my best self.* Again, these small internal changes eventually create great results in the external world later on.

So, serve yourself first, pay attention to the small things that you're integrating, notice how you are acquiring spiritual integrity through these small acts, and identify your skills and specialties so that these virtues from the Divine can work through you.

EXTENDING SEVA TO OTHERS

When you become peaceful within yourself, you can then begin to create peace in the world. How and where do you begin?

The initial steps are taken on a grassroots level, and I would say the focus is on quality, not quantity, helping one person or group of people at a time. If you see something that needs to be fixed, fix it. If something's broken, help to repair it. If someone needs money, donate a few or more dollars.

There are countless ways to give seva, but the most important aspect is remembering that you're bringing the energy of spiritual love into everything that you're called to do. In my community, we love to do what we call yogic farming. It's not just planting vegetables to eat healthily; it's about extending loving vibrations while we're doing it, and knowing that our crops can be of service to our neighbors and community. You see, sometimes we think that seva means we need to solve world hunger or save entire rain forests.

Again, start small and grow from there. The fact that you share a crop of vegetables with your neighbors is seva. Donating your used yet still good clothing to the homeless shelter is seva. Giving financial support to families who have been devastated by a tornado or flood is seva. Picking up a piece of paper when walking along a city street and putting it in the garbage can is seva. Teaching our young children a simple skill or trade is seva. Taking care of your elderly parent is seva. Even giving a smile to the cashier at your local store is seva.

The essence of seva is sensing a need, and doing something that you know will be of benefit to the other person or persons. It's doing whatever is necessary to make the world a kinder, better place. It starts right where you are. Just by your mere presence and expression, you can be of service.

When our energies are all focused on being a better version of ourselves and extending help to others, there's a magic that happens. The world improves even when we go our separate ways and do our respective service, but when we're together doing it, something is being invented that elevates the entire world . . . and there's something Divine in that.

Even though we're all different as individuals, there is something very pure at heart in showing up for others even with our differences, whether your work is building a house or running a prison or taking care of patients in the hospital. That purity amplifies through the desire to give first to others, and not take from them.

This is when the purpose of meditation expands to having the power to save not only our own lives, but to save humanity.

FINAL THOUGHTS AND BLESSINGS

—••●●••—

With the consistent integration of meditation and contemplation into our lives, the qualities of patience, cooperation, empathy, and forgiveness come forth, and it changes humanity in the most Divine ways. The ultimate benefit of these practices is that we get a more mature society. We begin to actually *live*, instead of keeping the soul trapped in societal, health, financial, political, and other problems that drain our strongest internal resource.

Although the way things are evolving in the world may appear to look tragic, these times are an invitation to all of humanity to claim back our Spirit. The ultimate reason why we are here—in these bodies, on this earth—is to reveal the Divinity of God's beauty through our individual choices, actions, behaviors, and relationships. Until we fully realize this, there will always be a depletion of our life force. So, it's important to consistently ask yourself, *How and where am I exhausting my soul's capacity and potential?* It takes alert awareness to pull the power from deep inside of you, and that's where meditation is invaluable. It has nothing to do with the outside, actually. Everything you need is inside of you.

Throughout time and within the last 100 years, survival took the form of food, shelter, and clothing, and these things are still essential. Yet there was something that we had and utilized more fully hundreds of years ago: an innate spiritual power. In this post-modern world, our spiritual power has been drained out of the soul through a variety of trivial distractions. Here we are, with technology, social media and so much at our disposal. Everything is available to us, which can be good—or not. If we become overly attached to these things, they will continue to deplete us of our vital spiritual energy, and the future is not going to be gentle with us.

How do we create a beautiful future in which we don't just exist and survive, but rather thrive and *fully live* beyond our wildest imaginings, and help others thrive, as well? The answer lies in building our internal spiritual strength through mastering the concepts of self-reflection and contemplation. This foundational attribute of hearing the Divine inside is what will grace us with equanimity when change occurs, which it will. On the road ahead, we will likely see that many of the things we once believed to be important and valuable, will be things that we have no interest in whatsoever. Incredible as it may seem now, they will no longer be useful to us.

This shift in perspective is all part of our positive evolution, to be able to see through illusions that we've upheld and have even gone to war for, and to have the presence to say, *Why are we even doing this? We don't need to do this anymore.* Even ideologies that we once entertained, we may no longer have the interest to sustain because, if we do, we will know that we're being untrue to ourselves. And perhaps the greatest benefit of this inward, mystical journey that meditation takes us on—as I've stated throughout these chapters—is the joy of experiencing your own sweet homecoming.

I believe that every soul who is listening inwardly, through contemplation and meditation, is currently getting the signals for and direction on what to let go of, what to nurture, and what to forgive. If we listen deeply, intuitively, and honestly, to the point of forgiving ourselves first, then we can reach a spiritual state where we are consciously detached from the interpretations connected to our five senses. Finally, we will become okay with being attached to the consciousness of our values, our virtues, and our spiritual potential, *as* we express ourselves through the five senses.

The more we use the tools of contemplation and meditation, and are able to feel the Divine in an intimate, experiential way, the closer we are to actually enjoying the bliss of existing in Life, of having Spirit flow through us.

The future wants to see human beings emanating Divine Love, compassion, and purity in our lives. It is thirsting to see a civilization of individuals who have the curiosity and courage to stand tall in their fullest essence of love, respect, dignity, and forbearance. The choice is ours to make. We can allow the future to be unkind to us . . . or we can choose a future that's bright by bringing in Divine light through our attitudes, personalities, actions, and choices. We can run our companies with that attitude. We can run our ashrams with that attitude. We can take care of our families with that attitude. We can run our schools, our countries, our world with that attitude.

We are in these bodies to live out the mystery of our Creator's loving vibration through us. Once we achieve that, my friends, we will have created heaven on earth.

MEET OUR SACRED STORYTELLERS

REV. DR. TERRLYN L. CURRY AVERY (TLC) is the creator of Pastology, the cutting-edge field that focuses on the synergy between pastoring and psychology. She is an ordained Presbyterian minister, author, coach, and host of the radio show *Dismantle Racism with Rev. Dr. TLC*.

EILEEN BILD is a talk show host, author, internationally syndicated columnist, and CEO of Ordinary to Extraordinary Life, and OTEL Universe. She has a master's degree in transpersonal psychology.

JANET CINCOTTA, M.D. is an author and physician with more than 30 years of experience in family medicine. She now occupies an empty nest, where she writes for the pure joy of it.

DIANNE COLLINS is the creator of QuantumThink and award-winning author of the bestselling *Do You QuantumThink? New Thinking That Will Rock Your World*. She is an acclaimed leader of new consciousness, popular media personality, and strategic consultant to executives and celebrities.

SEANA A. COUGHLIN is a reiki master, angel card reader, intuitive grief coach (through her company Conscious Grief), and ambassador of compassion with a master's degree in education and 20 years in the field of special education. Seana has two adult children—one in Heaven and one on Earth. She lives in Brooklyn, New York.

SUJON DATTA is an internationally renowned life architect, bioenergetic healer, and spiritual advisor. His mission is to help people open their hearts to themselves in order to reach their highest potential. He is related to Paramahansa Yogananda.

DR. ANN DINAN is an ICF-certified leadership coach and consultant who works globally in the corporate, government, and NGO sectors. Her passion is to align purpose and daily work.

PUJA SUE FLAMM is the author of *Restorative Yoga with Assists: A Manual for Teachers and Students of Yoga* and *93 Prescriptions for Joy: Cultivating Moments of Joy and Inner Peace*. She has been teaching yoga around the world for more than 35 years.

CAROLE D. FONTAINE, aka the "sailing yogi", lived on a sailboat for 20 years. Her bestselling memoir, *SAIL Above the Clouds,* shares adventures and inspiring tips for living a purposeful, engaging life.

ARIELLE FORD is the author of 11 books, including the international bestseller *The Soulmate Secret: Manifest the Love of Your Life with the Law of Attraction.* She has been called "The Cupid of Consciousness" and "The Fairy Godmother of Love."

ATHINA GEORDIN has been a spiritual seeker since her teens. She has lived in India for seven years, where she has experienced many enlightening encounters with spiritual masters who helped her find her true self.

REV. DR. STACY GOFORTH is the senior minister for The Interfaith Temple. She is a mystic, intuitive, author, coach, and speaker who encourages and guides seekers on their spiritual journeys. Her remarkable journey from evangelical Christianity to Interfaith ministry was sparked by a life-altering awakening experience.

DIANE L. HAWORTH is a heart-centered success coach, speaker, author, TV host, and founder of the Be Love Principles. She helps heart-centered leaders find clarity, calm, and confidence by consciously connecting to the Divine within. dianehaworth.com and beloveprinciples.org.

REV. TEMPLE HAYES is founder of the Institute for Leadership and Lifelong Learning International, and CEO of First Unity Spiritual Campus. She is a difference maker, spiritual leader, and author.

PHILIP M. HELLMICH is the former Director of Peace at The Shift Network and a member of the Evolutionary Leaders. He is the author of *God and Conflict: A Search for Peace in a Time of Crisis*.

JENNIFER HERRERA has been practicing energetic healing arts and bodywork for more than 10 years. She is a reiki master and a certified coach through HeartMath.

EMILY HINE is a technology, mental health, and mindfulness executive. She is a compassion teacher and author of *Holy Sit: Learning to Sit, Stay, Heal, and Serve*.

CHARLIE HOGG is Director of the Brahma Kumaris in Australia. He has been a daily meditator for 46 years and has traveled to nearly 100 countries. Charlie lives in Sydney.

DR. CHRISTINE E. KIESINGER is a speaker, author, trainer, personal and professional development coach, and founder of CEK Communication. She teaches exemplary leadership, conscious communication, emotional intelligence, integrative wellbeing, and mindfulness.

ARUNA LADVA has been a meditation teacher for more than 35 years. She has authored eight books and travels the world delivering lectures and conducting retreats on self-development. itstimetomeditate.org

JENAI LANE is the founder of Spirit Coach Training and author of *Spirit Led Instead*. An award-winning entrepreneur, intuitive coach, and trainer, she certifies coaches in a method to be spirit-led.

MARGO LENMARK is a relationship coach, author, and public speaker who has taught Transcendental Meditation and stress management in Egypt, India, Slovakia, and the Czech Republic. She is author of the highly acclaimed *Light in the Mourning: Memoirs of an Undertaker's Daughter*.

JEAN HOUSTON, PH.D. is a scholar, philosopher, and researcher in human capacities. She is one of the foremost visionary thinkers and doers of our time. Jean has long been regarded as one of the principal founders of the Human Potential Movement. Jean's story herein is excerpted from her autobiography, *A Mythic Life: Learning to Live Our Greater Story*.

SISTER JAYANTI has been a spiritual teacher for more than 50 years. She is the Additional Administrative Head and European Director of the Brahma

Kumaris, an international NGO of the United Nations that has been accredited with General Consultative Status with the UN's Economic and Social Council (ECOSOC).

KANU KOGOD, PH.D., M.C.C. is an anthropologist and executive coach who works with organizations on mindfulness and inclusion. She has been practicing meditation for more than 50 years, following the path of Kashmit Shaivism.

IRINA MORRISON assists others in improving their wellbeing, and discovering the essence of yoga and themselves. She weaves her skills in business and counseling to create experiences of transformation, relaxation, and rejuvenation for the body, mind, and soul.

KEN O'DONNELL is the director for the Brahma Kumaris World Spiritual University in South America. He is an experienced consultant who helps others approach common challenges from a humane perspective.

ANA-LA-RAI is a universal channel who brings forth the newest and highest energies, processes, activations, and messages. She offers teachings and healings through love, integrity, and unity consciousness in co-creation with the Guides and clients. She lives in gratitude on Vancouver Island with her husband.

YOGESH SHARDA is National Coordinator for the Brahma Kumaris in Turkey and works as a corporate trainer. He has been practicing Raja Yoga meditation since childhood.

BISHOP HEATHER SHEA is CEO and Spiritual Director for the United Palace of Spiritual Arts, Manhattan's fourth largest theater and a place where spirituality, art, and community unite.

REV. SYLVIA SUMTER is the senior minister for Unity of Washington, D.C. and founder of Stand Up for Humanity, as well as a teacher, speaker, and seeker of Truth. She is a contributing author of *Sacred Secrets: Finding Your Way to Joy, Peace, and Prosperity* and *Our Moment of Choice: Evolutionary Visions and Hope for the Future*. Sylvia received the 2020 New Thought Walden Awards for New Thought Wisdom.

DEBORAH LYN THOMPSON is a motivational speaker, world traveler, published author, and storyteller. She has been a student of the Brahma Kumaris since 1988, and inspires others with her *joie de vivre* after having had a near-death experience.

MAX TUCCI is an award-winning radio/TV host and personality, producer, author of *The Delmonico Way*, and truth seeker. Max's show *MAX & Friends* airs on various podcasting platforms.

SISTER VERONICA was raised in Ireland, has been an avid lifelong traveler, and is now based in Florida, where she continues to study and share the teachings of the Brahma Kumaris, which she connected with in 1976.

REV. CAROLYN WILKINS is the director of Agape's GlobalWorks Ministry, and the founding minister and spiritual director of Inspirational Ministries, a New Thought, ancient-wisdom, spiritual community in Las Cruces, New Mexico. inspirationalministries.org.

DR. TERESA VAN WOY is author of the award-winning and bestselling book *Wildflower: A Tale of Transcendence*. She lives in Benicia, California with her husband and three beautiful daughters, and enjoys traveling, photography, and woodworking.

KIMIA YAQUB is a poetic-mystic in heart and a spiritual researcher in mind. She was born and raised in Tehran, Iran.

MEET OUR FEATURED AUTHOR

SISTER DR. JENNA is an acclaimed, trusted spiritual mentor committed to bridging divides in societies and building relationships between global influencers. As the founder and director of the Brahma Kumaris Meditation Museum, located in the metropolitan Washington, D.C. area, she has impacted lives around the globe by inspiring change and finding solutions to current day crises.

Sister Dr. Jenna is the host of the popular America Meditating Radio Show and recipient of the President's Lifetime National Community Service Award. She is a member of the Evolutionary Leaders Circle, a group of thought leaders from diverse disciplines in service to conscious evolution and was selected by Empower A Billion Women 2020 as one of 100 most influential leaders of 2015.

Sister Dr. Jenna served as a partner with the Oprah Winfrey Network, and Values Partnerships on the Belief Team, a community of individuals from diverse spiritual, cultural, and faith backgrounds. She was awarded an Honorary Doctor of Humane Letters degree by St. Thomas Aquinas College in Sparkill, New York, for her many years of dedication to solving critical issues. Her mission is to continually build bridges, foster trust, decode critical current issues, and offer a perspective for folks to find clarity and inner power.

Sister Dr. Jenna has traveled to more than 93 countries offering tools and reflective methods for building community engagement and a more sustainable future. Her countless projects interconnect various sectors of society, leaving no life unmoved by her gentle and clear message for peace.

Learn more at americameditating.org and meditationmuseum.org.

CPSIA information can be obtained
at www.ICGtesting.com
Printed in the USA
FSHW020525030222
88107FS